Wallington

Northumberland

Raleigh Trevelyan

THE NATIONAL TRUST

Radical surprises

Many country houses are hidden from view by high walls, long drives or screens of trees. This is not the case with Wallington, which comes into sight a mile or more away on the roads from the south and south-west and again as one climbs the hill after crossing Paine's bridge. There is no majestic gateway, nor is there a lodge, which would have been out of keeping with the radical traditions of the families that have lived here. The exterior of the house is relatively unpretentious, but it must have seemed like an intrusion on the bare landscape when built by Sir William Blackett in the late 17th century. Even the front garden at first sight seems unexceptional. The surprises are the four griffins' heads grinning from the lawn – recovered originally by Sir Walter Calverley Blackett from Bishopsgate in London and brought by ship to Newcastle.

Splendour and seriousness

But there are other surprises. The present-day visitor passes under the elegant Palladian Clock Tower into the vast grassy courtyard. Then, as a complete contrast to the outside of the house, there is the exuberance of the Italian Rococo plasterwork in the main state rooms. From this 18th-century splendour one moves abruptly into a quite different atmosphere, more serious and intellectual, created by generations of the unconventional Trevelyans, who made Wallington famous for its associations with writers and scientists, Pre-Raphaelite painters and sculptors, actors and actresses, professors and politicians.

A secret garden

Then, there is the Walled Garden, half a mile from the house through the East Wood, opening up like a secret suddenly revealed. Developed with flowers and shrubs, rather than kitchen produce, by the National Trust, this garden still retains its intimacy and has colour all year round. On the terrace is the hot-house, typically Edwardian, with giant fuchsias, begonias and terracotta urns from Italy: a contrast once more.

The four griffins' heads on the lawn originally stood on Bishopsgate in the City of London. They were placed here by Mary (known as Molly), Lady Trevelyan, in 1928

Key figures

Sir William Blackett (c.1657–1705)

A wealthy Newcastle MP, merchant and mine-owner, he bought Wallington in 1688. He immediately pulled down the old Fenwick house and rebuilt it as four ranges around a central, open courtyard.

Sir Walter Calverley Blackett (1707–77)

A man of immense energy and taste, from about 1738 he commissioned the architect Daniel Garrett to modernise the house in the latest style, and decorate it with elaborate Italian plaster-work. He also transferred his mother's needlework decorations from Esholt, the Calverley house in Yorkshire.

Sir John Trevelyan, 5th Bt (1761–1846), and Maria, Lady Trevelyan (1772–1851)

Their marriage brought to Wallington much of the china collection and the Cabinet of Curiosities. They extended the Library, created the Museum Room, and altered rooms to house their growing family.

Sir Walter Calverley Trevelyan (1797–1879) and Pauline, Lady Trevelyan (1816–66)

Calverley and Pauline Trevelyan were a devoted couple who attracted to Wallington a fascinating circle of Victorian artists and intellectuals.

They employed John Dobson to roof over the courtyard to make the Central Hall and got William Bell Scott to decorate it with scenes from Northumbrian history. Calverley, as he was called, was the last member of the family to own both Wallington and the Nettlecombe estate in Somerset.

Sir Charles Edward Trevelyan, 1st Bt (1809–86)

Inherited Wallington from his cousin. With his second wife, Eleanora (1829–1919), he began refurnishing the house after the divided inheritance had left much of it empty. They united the entrance lobby and the china room to make the present Entrance Hall; this was the family's last major architectural change.

Sir George Otto Trevelyan (1838–1928)

He was an uncompromising politician and a distinguished historian in the mould of his uncle, Thomas Babington Macaulay, many of whose books survive in the Library. He and his wife, Caroline Philips (1849–1928), were much influenced by the Arts and Crafts movement and made extensive decorations to Wallington with William Morris furnishings.

Sir Charles Philips Trevelyan (1870–1958)

The eldest son of Sir George Otto, he was an even more radical politician than his father. He admired the early Soviet Union, joined the Labour Party and became its first education minister. Sharing his family's devotion to Wallington, on inheriting in 1928 he made extensive repairs to the house and introduced electricity. He opened the main rooms of the house from 1929, and published the first guidebook the following year. Determined to keep Wallington intact, he settled the estate on the National Trust in 1941.

Tour of the House

The Blackett family coat of arms, made from tubes of rolled paper – a technique known as quillwork

The Entrance Hall

Sir Walter Calverley Blackett made the entrance on the east side of the house in the early 1740s, but the Hall assumed its present form only in 1883, when Sir Charles Edward Trevelyan united the original narrow entrance passage with the separate parlour to the south, called the China Room. The paint colours used at this time, restored in 2003, show that he wanted the room to resemble a panelled hall in which hunting trophies would have been displayed. The room to the north of the passage was for 'Great Coats etc.' – very necessary here.

Pictures

The family portraits in the room include, over the fireplace, *Sir Charles Edward Trevelyan* (1809–86) by Rudolf Lehman (1878). Sir Charles, with his second wife, Lady Eleanora

Campbell, created this room. He was a model of the high-minded Victorian civil servant. Cousin of Sir Walter Calverley Trevelyan and brother-in-law of Macaulay, he was chosen to inherit Wallington by the former, and carried out the reforms in India advocated by the latter, as, successively, Governor of Madras (1859–60) and Finance Minister (1862–5).

The pair of portraits opposite on the south wall (by James Archer, 1871) are of Sir Charles's son *Sir George Otto Trevelyan* (1838–1928) and his wife, *Caroline Philips* (1849–1928); he always spoke of their marriage in 1869 as the most fortunate event of a fortunate life. She is shown with their eldest son (later Sir) *Charles Philips Trevelyan*, who gave Wallington to the National Trust. The recent posthumous portrait of Sir Charles opposite the front door is by his great-grandson, Jonathan Parker.

The *Blackett family coat of arms* was made about 1770 from pieces of rolled paper – a technique known as quillwork.

Furniture

Much of the furniture in the room was here over a century ago.

The mahogany armchairs are part of a set of

he Chippendale period. Such chairs with a distinctively wide and low profile are sometimes found in entrance halls. Slots in the bottom of the legs suggest that they could originally have been set on runners and used on soft lawns. Because of their squat appearance, they were nicknamed the 'Toads' by the family.

Ceramics

The Wallington collection of china, one of the most important owned by the National Trust, was brought to Wallington by the wife of Sir John Trevelyan, 5th Bt, *Maria Wilson*. Her portrait by R. C. Saunders after that by Hoppner (see Trevelyan Bedroom) hangs above the door beyond the fireplace. The displays here reflect their mixed character a hundred years ago. The long case facing the windows, built partly of Georgian woodwork, contains highly coloured *Italian maiolica* and other continental pieces, but mainly *oriental porcelain*, Chinese and Japanese.

The earliest pieces date from the late Ming Dynasty (early 17th-century), but most are of the Kangxi period (1662–1722). There is a fine series of vases, bowls and dishes decorated in *famille verte* (predominantly green) enamels. Here, too, are two *English delft punchbowls*, inscribed 'Lett us drink success to Blackett and Fenwick', probably made in Liverpool for the 1741 election which returned Sir Walter Blackett and Nicholas Fenwick as MPs for Newcastle. Alcohol was widely used to canvass support at 18th-century elections.

The Dutch marquetry cabinet on the south wall was moved, with its mixed contents, to this room in about 1933. It contains *English and continental porcelain*, including rare early Bow figures, Pulchinello and Harlequin, Chelsea pieces such as lemon tureens, and part of a Meissen tea service (see West Corridor). Here, too, as in the earlier mixture, are white Chinese figures.

(Left)
The English delft punch-bowls celebrate the election victory of Sir Walter Calverley Blackett in 1741

(Right)
Bow porcelain figures of Pulchinello and Harlequin, c.1752, characters from the Italian Commedia dell' Arte

The Dining Room

This room was always the Dining Room. Food had to be carried forty paces along the East Corridor from the Kitchen in the north-east corner of the ground floor. The screen of columns at the far end of the room separates the serving area from the diners.

Decoration

The decoration of the room was carried out for Sir Walter Blackett in 1740. The plasterwork, costing £23 19s 6d, was done by the Swiss-Italian stuccador Pietro Lafranchini.

In its Rococo maturity, the plasterwork here is as advanced as any in England. On the mirror frames, garlands are clutched in the beaks of double-headed eagles. Less dignified but more fun are the fish with shamrock tails crash-landing on to the outer edges of the frame above the chimneypiece. The four profile portraits of women at the corners of the ceiling are unidentified: were they Sir Walter's sisters? The most un-Georgian bearded head high on the west wall may be a later addition.

Appropriately for such a room, the relief panel in the ceiling beyond the screen shows a youthful Bacchus and friends enjoying a cask of wine. It was less appropriate for a family which championed temperance in the mid-19th century. The Wallington estate is still 'dry'.

The present decorative scheme, which follows the example of John Fowler elsewhere in the house, was designed by Peter Orde in the 1970s.

Pictures

The family portraits include (to the right of the fireplace) *Sir William Blackett* (*c.*1657–1705), the builder of Wallington; through the marriage in 1733 of his granddaughter, *Julia Calverley* (believed to be portrayed in the picture over the chimneypiece) to *Sir George Trevelyan, 3rd Bt* (left of fireplace, by Thomas Hudson) the Wallington estate passed to their son John in 1777.

Sculpture

The bronze bust at the window is of Sir Charles Philips Trevelyan, who settled Wallington on the National Trust; it was modelled by Gertrude Hermes.

Silver

On the dining-table is *a Rococo silver basket*, made by John Jacobs in London in 1750. It bears the arms of Calverley and Blackett, and the Calverley crest, an owl, on its swing handle.

Susanna (known as Sukey) Trevelyan (b.1736; over the sideboard) was painted in 1761 by Thomas Gainsborough, who originally depicted her in a more elaborate hat. This was painted over, reputedly by Reynolds, but you can still see traces of the wide rim. The changes were apparently made for her uncle, Sir Walter Calverley Blackett, who may have been influenced by Arthur Young's dismissive description of it as 'the *portrait of a hat and ruffles*'. Young's book is displayed below.

The tea-urn and tray on the Adam side-table were presented to Zachary Macaulay, the father of the historian and of Hannah, wife of Charles Edward Trevelyan, after the slave trade had been abolished in 1807, in recognition of his efforts to free the slaves. Josiah Wedgwood's design of a kneeling slave with the motto 'Am I not a man and a brother?' was engraved by the Northumbrian Thomas Bewick, better known for his book illustrations; the top boot is the crest of the Macaulays.

The Drawing Room

The Drawing Room, or Saloon, as it was called in the 18th century, stands directly over the vaulted basement of the Fenwicks' tower. This may have been to allow for a flagged floor, because for over 50 years, until the remodelling of 1740–1, this was the main entrance hall for the house. The original Baroque idea of a long straight drive up from the River Wansbeck to the front door probably proved too steep and was never completed. The room may have been entered originally from the central courtyard. So instead of a hall, this became the house's principal reception room. The ceiling was raised to allow for the drama of a great cove, and for a lavish display of plasterwork.

Decoration

As in the Dining Room, the decoration of the walls is concentrated around frames; again there are enigmatic faces, and this theme is continued above with sphinxes amongst Rococo curves abundant with vegetation and three-dimensional floral garlands and shells. By contrast, the central area of the ceiling, contained within a bold Greek key frame, relies for its effect on flatter patterns and more regular geometry. The decoration dates from 1741, the carpenter's bill being £56 17s 10d.

Originally, the ovals that flank the overmantel contained looking-glasses matching those on the window wall. The room was redecorated in 1885. Thereafter the family always called this the Drawing Room (and still do).

'The drawing room was used for larger and more formal gatherings, and for music. Two grand pianos stood under the big portrait of Sir Walter Blackett. As Lady Trevelyan [her mother] was a fine pianist, we made a good deal of music, playing on two pianos or singing to her accompaniment. My father had a noble tenor voice and from our early years used to sing the Harrow School songs to us'.

Pauline Dower

A master plasterer

In the 1760s Elizabeth, Duchess of Northumberland attributed the plasterwork to one 'Francini' – evidently, Pietro Lafranchini, who also decorated the Long Gallery of Northumberland House in London for her in 1750–4, and who was employed by several other patrons of Daniel Garrett. Pietro was the brother of Paolo and Filippo Lafranchini, who were working in Ireland at this time, and whose plasterwork in the gallery at Carlton, Co. Kildare, is very similar to the Wallington Drawing Room.

The present colouring of the walls dates from 1968 and was devised by John Fowler to complement that of the ceiling, which was cleaned then. Scrapes revealed that the walls, originally stone-coloured, were also once a lilac blue with the ornament white, but if this had been repeated, it was felt that the effect would have been overpowering and so it was decided to reverse the colours, making the walls white and the ornament lilac.

Chimneypiece

Attributed to Sir Henry Cheere (1703–81). The relief above it is copied from Andrea Schiavone's painting *The Judgement of Midas*, now at Hampton Court: King Midas (centre) judges Pan (below centre) a better musician than Apollo (left); for his temerity, Midas has his ears turned into those of an ass.

Picture

The room is dominated by the grand full-length portrait of *Sir Walter Calverley Blackett* (1707–77), painted by Joshua Reynolds about 1759–61. He had inherited Wallington in 1728 and much of the character of the estate today derives from his vision and drive. His businesslike north country clothes suggest the man of action he was. Roads were realigned, woods planted, farms improved. The setting of the house was enhanced with stable ranges, a clocktower coach-house, ponds and gardens, gate-

ways and sculpture. Woods framed southern views over parkland to the Wansbeck valley with Paine's classical bridge. He also made many changes to the house, and, not least, this room was created for him.

Ceramics

On the carpet stands a large *Chinese famille rose fishbowl*, on a gilt mahogany stand, which was already here by the 1760s, when Arthur Young described it as 'a noble china cistern'. The inside is appropriately decorated with fish.

Textiles

The needlework panel, in the plaster frame on the east wall for which it was designed, was embroidered by Mary, Lady Trevelyan in 1910–33. It illustrates the legend of the 'first' Trevelyan, who is said to have swum his horse from St Michael's Mount to the mainland of

Cornwall for a wager. The four shields are those of families connected with Wallington: the Fenwick red and white martlets; the Blackett mullets and scallops; the Trevelyan horse rising from the waves; and the hawk's bells and lures of Lady Trevelyan's family, the Bells. 'Tyme Tryeth Troth' is the Trevelyan motto, and the owl is the crest of the Calverleys.

The Chinese famille rose fishbowl, which has been in this room since at least the 1760s

The Library

Decoration

The Library was the drawing room in Sir Walter Blackett's time and was decorated in 1741, again with plasterwork by Lafranchini and with a chimneypiece probably by Cheere (now with a Victorian cast-iron grate with De Morgan tiles). In 1816 the west wall was replaced with the Ionic column screen and new cornice (designed by John Dobson?), and the space beyond, originally a corridor leading to closets, was incorporated into the room.

In 1853 Sir Walter Trevelyan refitted the room as a library, obscuring a decorative scheme which included rust-coloured flock wallpaper. The paper, where exposed, had been painted. This paint colour was restored in 2003, when the ceiling was repaired and cleaned. Cracks in the ceiling, long believed to have been related to the location beneath the family nursery, may have been caused partly by the addition of dividing walls above.

Books

During the 19th and 20th centuries, the Trevelyans were prolific writers and avid readers. Their library of over 3,000 books

'Of an evening, gathered in the library after supper, we played games, all together, not in small groups – cards of various sorts, including Racing Demon, letter games, Mah Jong, charades, guessing games or general knowledge. Or my father would read aloud to us, and in school holidays there would be a great variety of books being used, to suit all ages.'

Pauline Dower

reflects this, and is one of the most interesting in the care of the National Trust. It is especially rich in 19th-century history, politics, classics, literature and topography. More unusually, the library also contains such rare early cookery books as *The Complete House-Keeper & Professed Cook* (1772). The volumes on Northumberland belonged to Sir Walter Calverley Trevelyan, who helped John Hodgson with his history of the county. A gilt 'M' on the spine identifies over 500 books that came from the library of the historian Lord Macaulay, whose sister married Sir Walter's cousin and successor at Wallington.

Many of the books bear witness to the family habit of making marginal comments on the author's opinions, style and syntax – even Shakespeare did not escape brisk criticism. There are also numerous author's presentation copies, including two from Queen Victoria. Sir Charles Philips Trevelyan encouraged local people and friends to borrow books from here.

Pictures

Over the chimneypiece, the *Landscape with classical ruins* evokes the golden light and ancient remains of southern Italy, but it was painted by a French artist, Pierre-Antoine Patel the Younger, in the late 17th century. Its superb Rococo frame relates happily to Lafranchini's plasterwork above. The picture serves as a reminder that the Grand Tour was an important part of young gentlemen's education. The small picture by the Study door of *Luther leaving Augsburg* is by an imitator of Lucas Cranach.

Furniture

The comfortable leather-covered library furniture includes an armchair with a built-in bookstand. The large desk is that at which Lord Macaulay wrote his *History of England* (1849–55).

Sculpture and clock

The grand marble bust by the window is of the historian *Thomas Babington, Lord Macaulay* by Patric Park. *The bronze profile of Macaulay* was sculpted by Carlo Marochetti in 1848.

The bronze statuettes of the French Enlightenment thinkers *Voltaire* and *Rousseau* were presented to Lord Macaulay by Lady

Holland in memory of her husband. The latter appears, with the *du Chesne clock*, also here, in E. M. Ward's painting of Macaulay in his study (a reproduction is displayed here).

The Study

When Sir William Blackett built the house, the main staircase was here, rising in three flights around a square well. This was removed in 1743 by Daniel Garrett for Sir Walter Blackett, who made the room into an ante-room to the main west bedchamber.

Both Sir George Otto and Sir Charles Philips Trevelyan used the room as a study, and it now contains many small portraits, photographs and other mementoes of the Trevelyans.

Pictures

The small oval portraits, between the windows, of *Sir Walter Calverley Trevelyan* (1797–1879) and *Pauline, Lady Trevelyan* (1816–66), were probably painted during their extended honeymoon in Italy, in 1835–8.

Furniture

The writing-table at which Sir George Otto Trevelyan wrote his *History of the American Revolution* (1899–1909).

The honours in the glass-topped cabinet include the Orders of Merit conferred on Sir George Otto (1911) and George Macaulay Trevelyan (1930), the only instance of father and son being so honoured.

'I used often to sit with [her grandfather, George Otto Trevelyan] in the study, listening absorbed while he read aloud Homer in Greek from uncle Tom Macaulay's great library copy. He would read a page and then go back and translate it for me, and in this way I got to know the great stories of the Iliad and Odyssey, the siege of Troy and Ulysses' long voyage home to his final triumph, a wonderful way to hear these great epics.'
Pauline Dower

Lady Trevelyan's Parlour

Throughout the Georgian period this room continued to be used as the principal bedchamber. As it occupies such an important position in the centre of the west front, it was probably that usually occupied by Sir Walter Blackett. From the 1880s it was used as a sitting-room by successive Ladies Trevelyan: Eleanora moved here when the old parlour became the Entrance Hall and established this room as a ladies' retreat; Caroline introduced the Morris wallpaper in 1897; and Molly purchased the carpet at the Morris & Co. closing-down sale in 1940.

The room, which became known as the Parlour, contains part of the family's rich collection of 19th-century pictures.

Pictures

They include works by J. M. W. Turner, Lord Leighton and David Cox. Walter James's striking view of the *Carrara Mountains* above the fireplace is flanked by portraits of (left) *Sir Charles Edward Trevelyan as a youth*, who was painted about 1825 in a romantic Byronic pose, around a year after the poet's death, when the Byron cult was still at its height; and (right) his grandson *Robert Calverley Trevelyan,* who was a poet, painted by Aubrey Waterfield.

Opposite the chimneypiece is Edward Burne-Jones's *The Pilgrim at the Gate of Idleness*, derived from the second of five scenes depicting the *Romaunt of the Rose* (an allegory of the pursuit of love once attributed to Chaucer and very popular with Pre-Raphaelite artists), which was designed by Burne-Jones and William Morris in 1874 to be embroidered by Margaret Bell and her daughter Florence as a needlework frieze for their dining room at Rounton Grange in Yorkshire. The drawing, which was made in the 1870s but

worked over again by Burne-Jones in the 1890s was acquired in 1904 by Charles Philips Trevelyan as a birthday present for Margaret's granddaughter, Molly, whom he had married the same year.

Flanking the picture are two portraits by William Bell Scott: *Sir Walter Calverley Trevelyan, 6th Bt* (1797–1879) was painted in 1859 in the Drawing Room, sitting next to the Chinese *famille rose* bowl, which is still in the room; and *Pauline Trevelyan* in 1864 holding camellias picked from plants she had acquired in Portugal in 1846. The Trevelyans had commissioned Scott to decorate the Central Hall in 1855. To the left are Turner watercolours

(Right) Molly Trevelyan working on her needlework panel illustrating the legendary origin of the Trevelyan family. The panel itself (illustrated on p. 40) is now displayed in the Drawing Room

(Above) The Pilgrim at the Gate of Idleness; by Edward Burne-Jones (Lady Trevelyan's Parlour)

of two romantic Northumbrian ruins, *Dunstanburgh Castle* and *Brinkburn Priory*.

The group of pictures between the windows relates to John Ruskin's friendship with Pauline Trevelyan and his role as drawing teacher. The small square *Italian landscape* by Ruskin was to demonstrate Renaissance painting. The *Swiss Alps* are shown in watercolour by Pauline and drawings by Ruskin, including one of her grave. William Bell Scott's watercolour, *John Ruskin teaching Louisa Stewart-Mackenzie to draw*, 1857, reflects his jealousy of the adoration Ruskin received from Pauline Trevelyan and many of her women friends, like Louisa Stewart-Mackenzie. He was also critical of Ruskin's teaching methods, which entailed beginning in a top corner and finishing each section as one went along – 'next to impossible', he thought.

The pastel double portrait of Elsa and Mary Bell was painted by Lady Caroline Grosvenor in 1899. Five years later, Mary married Charles Philips Trevelyan. Elsa and Mary were the daughters of the Middlesbrough ironmaster Sir Hugh Bell, of Rounton Grange, an enlightened patron of Arts and Crafts artists.

A full handlist of the pictures is available in the room.

Furniture

The mahogany chest-of-drawers is an unusual type of mid-18th-century butler's chest, with recessed handles, possibly used for travelling. It contains four drawers fitted to take wine bottles.

Ceramics

The case by the Hall door contains a variety of Wallington's best china including examples of Bow, Chelsea, Sèvres, Dutch Delft and early Meissen.

*The Madonna and Child;
attributed to Francesco Francia
(West Corridor)*

*(Below)
Meissen porcelain coffee service,
decorated by J. G. Klinger,
c.1740–45*

The West Corridor

Here and in the East Corridor the walls and
vaults were repainted in 2004 with the original
colours, terracotta brown and light stone.
The flagged floors, extensively damaged by
damp, were replaced. Fragments of the original
red Italianate carpet runner had survived, and a
replica was made.

Ceramics

In the Sheraton display case is the **Meissen
porcelain tea and coffee service** decorated with
remarkably precise shadowed insects in the style
of J. G. Klinger (1711–81), c.1740–5. Either this

et was ordered by Sir Walter Blackett about 1740–5, or it was brought to the house by Sir John Trevelyan, 5th Bt, around 1817. Portraits of both hang nearby.

Pictures

Facing the Central Hall: *The Madonna and Child*, attributed to Francesco Francia (1450–1517) and Studio, is the only survivor of a good small collection of Italian Renaissance painting and sculpture belonging to the Trevelyans. It is exactly the kind of Italian Old Master picture that was admired by those, like Calverley and Pauline Trevelyan, with a taste for the Pre-Raphaelites, although it was in fact acquired much later, by Sir George in 1899.

Sculpture

Over the Parlour door: Alexander Munro's relief profile portrait of *Sir Walter Calverley Trevelyan*, who created the Central Hall with his wife *Pauline* (see north-east pier).

Over the Writing Room door is Alexander Munro's plaster *Repose: Study of a Babe*. The baby sleeps among hyacinths, which symbolise premature death: in Greek legend the beautiful young boy Hyacinthus was accidently killed by Apollo, and the flowers sprang from his blood. The connection was made most

Sir Walter Calverley Trevelyan; by Alexander Munro

famously by Milton in his poem 'On the Death of a Fair Infant'.

The *bronze putti*, or winged boys, on marble columns were brought from Italy by Sir George Otto Trevelyan in 1898, to be 'at home' in the Italianate hall.

The Writing Room

Originally, the southern half of this room served as a bed closet to the principal bedchamber. By 1740 it had become simply the Dressing Room. The room was extended, and used as a billiard room, when a staircase to its north was removed in the later 19th century. The new room straddled the line between the family part of the house and the domestic quarters, with one door to the Central Hall and the other to the servants' corridor and back door. The window over the latter allows light into the servants' corridor. The convenience of this arrangement influenced Sir Charles Philips Trevelyan to use the room as his estate office from the early 1930s.

The room has been arranged to provide you with a place in which to sit down and rest, and to write. Letters may be posted in the table post-box.

Maps and pictures

The estate maps trace the development of Wallington from 1728 to the 20th century. Here, too, are shown in rotation selections from the house's rich collection of *architectural and landscape designs, and watercolour drawings*.

Furniture

The 18th-century *architect's table* between the doors has a double rising top and a drawer fitted to take drawing materials, which pulls out on supporting legs and has a baize-covered reading slide.

Textiles

The needlework panel of the estate, above the fireplace, was worked by Pauline Dower, eldest daughter of Sir Charles Philips Trevelyan. It still belongs to the family, but is generously lent to be shown in the house each visiting season.

The Central Hall

The Hall was designed by John Dobson of Newcastle to enclose the originally open central courtyard. It was built in 1853–4. In step with early Victorian fashion, an historic style was chosen to be in accord with the room's modern purpose. Reflecting the Trevelyans' wish that Wallington should be a centre for intellectual, artistic and scientific pursuits, Dobson created for them the courtyard of an Italian Renaissance palazzo. John Ruskin, of course, supported the scheme, and the balustrade is even copied from plate xiii in the second volume of his *The Stones of Venice* (1853), which illustrates medieval details from Murano Cathedral.

Decoration

In March 1856 William Bell Scott, director of the Newcastle School of Design and a friend of the Pre-Raphaelite D. G. Rossetti, was commissioned by Calverley and Pauline Trevelyan to decorate Dobson's new palazzo courtyard with 'wall paintings'. His brief was 'to illuminate the

'The central hall was the hub of the house. It was carpeted and we always had tea at a big refectory table which stood along the south side of the hall. The big toys – rocking horses of various sizes, big wooden bricks, the larger toys now in the nursery – were kept in the hall, which was very much the children's playroom.'

Pauline Dower

history and worthies of Northumbria'. For the lower register between the piers of the north and south walls he painted on canvases about 1.87 m square eight tableaux illustrating the history of the region, from the building of Hadrian's Wall to the industrial achievements of mid-19th-century Tyneside. In accordance with Pre-Raphaelite precepts, Scott took immense trouble to get the historical and natural details right.

Furthering the idea of this being an open courtyard, flowers and plants were included in the painted decoration. For the piers in the lower register, which run round all four sides of the Hall, Scott proposed groups of tall, principally native plants like foxgloves and bulrushes. They were to be painted with naturalistic precision, again in oil directly on to the stone. Pauline was responsible for many of these, but she also managed to persuade others to contribute; even Ruskin was recruited to paint the group of wild oats, wheat, cornflowers and yarrow in the south-west corner.

The keystones of the arches are shaped as cartouches bearing family coats of arms. In Renaissance style, the lower spandrels (areas between the arches) were embellished with medallion portraits of the eminent, in this case those famous in Northumbrian history, from Hadrian to George Stephenson.

In 1863 Scott was commissioned to fill the upper spandrels with the story of the battle of Otterburn in 1388 from the Border ballad *Chevy Chase*.

Sculpture

Thomas Woolner's *Civilisation* depicts a mother teaching her young son to recite the Lord's Prayer. Woolner chose a woman as teacher, because 'the position of women in society always marks the degree to which the civilisation of the nation has reached'. The child stands on a plinth carved, by contrast, with scenes of pagan savagery. Sculpted between 1856 and 1867, it was intended to provide the focal point for the Central Hall.

Alexander Munro carved the high-relief tondo of *Pauline, Lady Trevelyan* set into the north-east pier.

The Bell Scott Paintings

Building the Roman Wall

The setting is near the Roman fort of Housesteads (Borcovicum) and Crag Lough, and shows the half-built Hadrian's Wall under attack by Caledonians (right background). The Roman centurion rebukes the man lounging in the foreground, who is hiding dice under his right hand. For greater realism Scott used contemporary portraits and borrowed actual Wall stones to copy. Painted January–June 1857.

King Egfrid and St Cuthbert

Egfrid, King of Northumbria, and Bishop Theodore (centre) came to the Farne Islands in 684 to ask Cuthbert to exchange his spade (he had been digging onions) for the crozier and become Bishop of Hexham. Cuthbert reluctantly agreed, but shortly afterwards exchanged the see for that of the more remote Lindisfarne. He resigned two years later to return to his hermit's cell. Painted June–December 1856.

The Descent of the Danes

A band of marauding Danish Vikings lands out of the spring morning mist near Tynemouth Rock, while the local inhabitants prepare hastily to repel them. The woman in profile at the top of the cliff is a portrait of Pauline Trevelyan; at her feet is her favourite dog, Peter. Painted January–June 1858.

The Death of Bede

The Venerable Bede, to whom we owe much of our knowledge of early English history, died at Jarrow Priory on 26 May 735. He lived just long enough to complete his translation of St John's Gospel into Anglo-Saxon. The blown-out candle, the dove flying from the window, and the hour-glass all symbolise the passing of life. Painted June–December 1857.

The Spur in the Dish

The mistress of the house brings in a spur on a dish to tell her menfolk that they must ride out to replenish the larder. This medieval Border legend is associated with the Charltons of Hesleyside. The interior is based on the keep of Newcastle Castle.
Painted August 1858–January 1859.

Bernard Gilpin

The setting is nearby Rothbury church *c.*1570. Bernard Gilpin takes down a gauntlet that had been hung in the church as a challenge in a feud between two local families (shown in the foreground) and makes peace between them. The man standing at the lectern is a portrait of Sir Walter Trevelyan, who owned the original gauntlet and would have strongly endorsed the theme of this scene: 'Blessed are the peace-makers for they shall be called the children of God.' The man on the extreme left is William Bell Scott himself.
Painted January–August 1859.

Grace Darling

On 7 September 1838 the steamer *Forfarshire* was wrecked a mile from the Longstone lighthouse on the Farne Islands. Grace Darling, with her father William, the lighthouse keeper, rowed through the storm to rescue the surviving passengers and became a model of female heroism for the Victorians. The woman passenger sheltering in the left foreground is a portrait of Bell Scott's mistress, Alice Boyd.
Painted January–October 1860.

In the 19th century the Northumbrians show the world what can be done with Iron and Coal

An imaginary compilation celebrating Newcastle's industrial prowess in the 1860s. The four men on the right are hammering a red-hot iron wheel into shape and were based on studies made in Robert Stephenson's railway engine works. The left-hand worker is a portrait of Charles Edward Trevelyan, the heir to Wallington. Below is a design for one of the factory's most recent locomotives. The anchor and ship's airpump next to it were made by another local firm, Hawks, Crawshay. The final scene in the series, completed in June 1861.

The Servants' Hall

This room is the Servants' Hall of the original house. It has older windows and glazing bars than the others, and possibly its original cornice. The room now contains a collection of dolls' houses.

> 'The whole indoor staff gathered for meals there, but after the meat course the housekeeper and the butler would rise and go to the housekeeper's room ... for the second course, leaving either the lady's maid or the head housemaid in charge of the servants' hall.'
>
> Pauline Dower

Dolls' houses

Hammond House, in the centre, is a model mansion of some 36 rooms, each lit by electric light. All the wallpapers and floor coverings are original, and so are the furniture, china, glass, linen and cutlery. The 77 dolls have china faces and range from the master and mistress of the house through a large family and a full staff of servants, and provide an interesting record of life in such a house in the 1880s. The name comes from the fact that 'Ruby Hammond' appears on a tiny towel and in a miniature copybook. It was discovered in the 1960s in a York antique shop by Sheila Pettit, former Historic Buildings Representative for Northumbria.

Twelve of the other houses form part of the Angus collection, which was assembled by Mrs Bridget Angus of Corbridge, a devoted

The library of Hammond House

supporter of the Trust, and was given to Wallington by her family on her death in 1973. The houses are mainly 19th-century in date and show an interesting range of styles throughout that period. All the contents were given with the houses.

The Children's Room

A storeroom leading off the Servants' Hall has been converted to accommodate the many gifts made to Wallington since the opening of the Nursery and Common Room, and is accessible only by means of a ladder attached to the wall. It contains many interesting old children's toys, games, china, books, a splendid Noah's Ark and a notable model of a monastery in Moscow. Adults may enter only when accompanied by a responsible child.

The North Corridor

The North Corridor gave servants discreet access from their working areas to the public and family rooms. The corridor was repainted in 2004 as it had been a century earlier. Because the area was darker, this was a lighter version of the main corridor colour.

The Servants' Common Room

The Common Room was strategically placed between the Kitchen and the north service stairs. Originally and principally used by the Housekeeper and other upper servants, it is decorated to reflect this status. It was part of the servants' area on the north side of the house which included a Butler's Pantry, Lamp Room, coal house, earth closet and pantries. This room is now used for occasional exhibitions and meetings.

Model soldiers

The collection of model lead soldiers, now totalling 3,800, was acquired in the early 1880s for the three sons of Sir George Otto Trevelyan – Charles, Robert and George. They were made in Germany.

The boys set them out on the floor of the Museum above the Saloon, following plans of actual battles of the Marlborough and Napoleonic wars. Books were used to represent hills. Careful calculations were made as to the correct fire-power of the guns and the agreed number of soldiers laid low at each volley; a battle might therefore take several days to complete.

It was to this study of the game of *Kriegsspiel* that G. M. Trevelyan attributed his own capacity for so vividly describing battles, and both he and Sir Charles gave *Kriegsspiel* as their hobby in *Who's Who*, even as adults.

The soldiers are today laid out in regiments of Napoleon's, Blücher's and Wellington's armies, exactly as Sir Charles left them in the Museum.

(Below) The Kitchen

The Kitchen

Arranged to look as it might have done about 1900, the Kitchen contains some of the contents that have always been at Wallington. The coal-fired stoves are replacements of similar design to the originals and were in use locally until 1970. The dresser and tables of scrubbed pine have seen many years of service in the house, as have the knife-cleaner and the pestle and mortar in the wall-fitting by the sink. The door on the north-east originally led to pantries and sculleries.

The great roof girder, made by Dorman Long of Middlesbrough, was inserted in 1928 to tie in the east wall. This was collapsing outwards and had to be partially rebuilt. The Kitchen was in use until 1967.

Thomas H. Kendall of Warwick's 1872 wood-carving of a mouse threatening a bird's nest (East Corridor)

The East Corridor

Wood carvings

The two carvings of flora and fauna were made in 1872 by Thomas H. Kendall of Warwick, then a thriving centre for this kind of ornate carving. They came from Welcombe, the Warwickshire home of Sir George Otto's wife, Caroline.

The Staircase Hall

The principal staircase was moved to what had been part of the central courtyard by Sir Walter Calverley Blackett in 1743. Some of the wood-work and plasterwork dates from that time. When the Central Hall was formed in 1853, the original ceiling was taken down and the staircase seems to have been rebuilt in stone then.

(Right) Paolo and Francesca; by Alexander Munro, 1851 (Staircase Hall)

Sculpture

Opposite the foot of the stairs, in the position it occupied for most of the second half of the 19th century, is Alexander Munro's intimate group of Dante's doomed lovers *Paolo and Francesca* (1851). This was inspired by Canto V of Dante's *Inferno*, in which Francesca da Rimini describes how she and her lover Paolo Malatesta read of the equally illicit passion of Lancelot for Guinevere:

As we read on, our eyes met now and then,
And to our cheeks the changing colour started,
But just one moment overcame us – when
We read of the smile, desired of lips long-thwarted,
Such smile, by such a lover kissed away,
He that may never more from me be parted
Trembling all over, kissed my mouth.

Her final words are inscribed in Italian on the base: 'We read no more that day.'

The portrait busts are of: *Spencer Perceval* (1762–1812) by Joseph Nollekens; he was Prime Minister from 1809 until 1812, when he was assassinated in the lobby of the House of Commons.

His wife was the sister of Maria, Lady Trevelyan; and *Dr Whewell*, a Cambridge friend of Calverley and Pauline. The splendid white marble *Athenian owls* are another continental souvenir of Sir George Otto.

Transport

The 17th-century Swiss 'dragon sleigh' (as it was always known to the Trevelyans) was originally mounted on large runners and could be towed around the garden by a horse. It was bought early in the 20th century by Mary, Lady Trevelyan.

Picture

John Wootton's *Dancing dogs* was painted in 1759. According to a letter of about 1767, Sir Walter Calverley Blackett's 'fondness for his little Dogs is quite ridiculous & Childish'. The startled jay in the picture shows that both patron and artist were perfectly aware of the dogs' absurdity. Identified underneath as Lusette, Madore, Rosette and Mouche, they are a diminutive French derivative (like the poodle) of the water spaniel, or barbel, close to today's bichon.

The Galleries

Pictures

The portraits hanging on the Galleries are mainly of members of the family, including daughters of Sir William Blackett, 1st Bt, who all found themselves rich husbands. In the middle of the East Gallery is *Sir John Trevelyan, 4th Bt* (1734–1828), painted by George Romney in 1784–8 with proud paunch and crossed legs – the mark of male elegance in the 18th century. Sir John inherited Wallington from his uncle, Sir Walter Blackett, in 1777, but preferred to live on his Somerset estate at Nettlecombe. This picture used to hang at Nettlecombe. It was bought by the National Trust in 1991 with generous help from the family and the National Art Collections Fund.

Dancing dogs; by John Wootton, 1759 (Staircase Hall)

Ceramics

In the Sheraton case on the East Gallery is a collection of *English and continental porcelain figures*, including early examples from the Bow, Chelsea, Longton Hall and Derby works. The figures of *nuns* are particularly instructive in showing how Meissen figures were very quickly copied by Chelsea and Bow artists. Most flamboyant, however, are the *Meissen groups symbolising four continents*, Europe, Asia, Africa and America. These were first modelled in 1745–6 by J. J. Kändler (1706–75), the greatest of the German porcelain modellers.

'A game in which all the family, old or young, joined was the Stocking Game, so-called because the "He" carried a pair of rolled-up golf stockings as ammunition and simply chased all the rest round the gallery until he hit someone with the stocking ball.... The noise was terrific, as you can imagine, but there were no casualties.'

Pauline Dower

The Lobby off the East Gallery

This small lobby gives access from the East Gallery to the central rooms of the east front. The pictures are a fascinating but confusing group of portraits of the Pye and Calverley families, some apparently incorrectly inscribed: *Sir Walter Pye*, 1631, by Cornelius Jonson (1593–1664/5?); he was a successful Herefordshire lawyer. His daughter married *Henry Calverley*, 1638, the 'brat at nurse' who escaped murder by his deranged father, Walter Calverley. The portrait inscribed 'Joyce Pye' is probably not Henry Calverley's wife, but his mother, *Philippa Calverley*, who holds a note with a message suggesting that by remaining silent at his trial for infanticide, Walter Calverley was prepared to be executed by pressing (the last person to suffer this fate) and by doing so, to preserve his estate from sequestration.

The Needlework Room

The Needlework Room is the most complete survivor from 18th-century Wallington, and was part of a suite of rooms created for Elizabeth, wife of Sir Walter Blackett.

Needlework

The ten panels of needlework were worked by Julia, Lady Calverley, in the 1710s for the drawing room at Esholt Hall, the Calverley seat

Julia, Lady Calverley (1686–1736), who created the needlework panels in the Needlework Room and the Pigeon Hole in the early 18th century

near Bradford which was copied from Wallington. They were brought to Northumberland in 1755 by Julia's son, Sir Walter Calverley Blackett, when he sold Esholt, and the Rococo frames in carved wood were presumably made at this time. The central panel on the north wall is dated 1717. The designs, which are carried out in wool and silk in tent-stitch, appear to have been influenced by oriental textiles imported into England in the late 17th and early 18th centuries. They took only three years to make, so Lady Calverley must have had assistance. Pauline Dower's painting of the reverse of a panel, made during repairs to the woodwork, gives an idea of the brilliance of the original colours.

The covers of the six chairs are stitched in a similar technique to match the panels, but there is no proof that Lady Calverley made them.

Pictures

The oval portraits were painted between about 1695 and 1709, and include images of Julia, Lady Calverley, who worked the panels in this room, and, as a baby, of her son, Sir Walter Calverley Blackett, 2nd Bt (1707–77), who created it. The original silvering of the frames has been restored. The repainting of the room, in original stone colours more harmonious with the needlework, is part of the current redecoration programme. It is being financed by the County Durham Centre of the National Trust.

The Pigeon Hole

This small room over the entrance lobby, in the awkward space between two chimneystacks, was previously shown as a bathroom; it now has the name by which the Trevelyans knew it.

Textiles and picture

The very fine six-leaf *needlework screen* was made in 1727 by *Julia, Lady Calverley*, whose portrait hangs on the north wall. It was worked in wool in fine *petit point*. Her inspiration for the scenes on the screen was Wenceslaus Hollar's engravings for the 1663 edition of the *Georgics* and *Eclogues* of the Roman poet Virgil.

The Blackett Bedroom

This room owes its name to the bed made about 1765, which belonged to Sir Walter Calverley Blackett, and to the portraits, predominantly of the Blackett family, which hang here.

Pictures

The early family portraits include Sir William Blackett, 1st Bt (*c.*1620–80), who founded the Blackett family's fortunes.

> ### Wallpaper
>
> Following a severe outbreak of dry rot, the room was redecorated in 1983. During the repair work fragments of the original early 18th-century wallpaper were revealed, and these can now be seen framed near the door. The design, like the panels in the Needlework Room, was influenced by imported oriental textiles. After a prolonged search, a similar design was found and reproduced by Katzenbach & Warren Inc. of New York, and the cost was met by the Durham Centre of the National Trust.

The Trevelyan Bedroom

The bedroom is approached through an ante-room busy with engravings, watercolours and family photographs. The main bedroom is one of four which appear to have been made from a long gallery that ran the full length of the south side of the house. Old-fashioned, this had been sacrificed in 1741, when the cove in the Saloon was raised. It was not until the early 19th century that Sir John and Maria, with a growing family, and new standards of privacy, started to make further divisions. In the mid-19th century Pauline used the room as her boudoir. Because of the morning light and views southwards, later generations chose it as the master bedroom.

Pictures

To the left of the group portrait above the fire-place is a portrait by John Hoppner of *Maria Wilson*, painted at the time of her wedding in 1791 to *Sir John Trevelyan, 5th Bt*, whose portrait of the 1780s by George Romney hangs to the right. The picture between the door and the bed shows three of their twelve *Children playing* in front of the Clock Tower; the boy is Walter Calverley, who succeeded his father and created the Central Hall. Above hangs a small but characterful portrait of Sir John's father, Sir John, 4th Bt, the first member of the Trevelyan family to own Wallington.

Furniture

The room is now dominated by *the mid-19th-century four-poster bed* that belonged to Lord Macaulay.

Panel from the needlework screen made in 1727 by Julia, Lady Calverley in the Pigeon Hole

The Nursery

The room was created about 1820 when the eastern remnant of a long gallery was divided into two. The same division was made on the west side of the house (now private) and in each case a door in the dividing wall allowed for continued communication between the two rooms. This was not the original nursery (which was on the west side of the house), but was decorated and arranged in 1969 with an assembly of objects and toys, some used by successive generations of Trevelyan children.

Textiles

Appliqué needlework panels, worked by Mary, Lady Trevelyan in 1906 and 1909 for the nursery at Cambo House, where she was living before her husband inherited Wallington in 1928.

Toys and dolls

Late 18th-century horse tricycle, propelled by the hands. Sir George Otto's grandchildren were allowed to play with it on Sunday afternoons, riding it around the Gallery. Of the wax- and china-faced dolls shown, the one dressed in black was the favourite possession of Caroline, Lady Trevelyan. The latest arrival is 'Jacky', Pauline Dower's teddy bear, with a pale green top and the small head characteristic of early teddies.

Lady Wilson's Cabinet of Curiosities

The collection was formed by Dame Jane Wilson of Charlton House, Greenwich (1749–1818), whose portrait hangs here. It was inherited by her daughter Maria, who married Sir John Trevelyan, 5th Bt, in 1791. They had set up the collection as a museum by 1827, when the Rev. John Hodgson described the contents of this room in his *History of Northumberland*.

Many of the things described by Hodgson are elsewhere in the house today, or have been given away by successive Trevelyans to various museums and universities. Much, however,

remains, and the room has been restored and rearranged to display it.

Picture

Dame Jane Wilson was the great-niece and heiress of the Rev. John Maryon of Charlton House, Greenwich (whose estates included most of what is now Hampstead Heath). Profoundly interested in natural history, Jane was a pioneering coleopterist (beetle expert) and formed the cabinet of curiosities. She holds a catalogue of this on her knee, open at the pages devoted to its best specimens, 'Shells' and 'China', and Charlton House is seen in the background.

Stuffed animals

The cases of stuffed birds are from the collection formed by Lady Wilson, and possibly added to by Sir Walter Calverley Trevelyan. They were both keen naturalists, and Sir John Trevelyan and Sir Walter corresponded with Thomas Bewick, the great Newcastle engraver and naturalist whose portrait was included among the Northumbrian worthies in the Central Hall. The backgrounds to the cases were painted by Pauline Dower in the 1970s.

Curiosities

The first wall-case on the left contains the remaining collection of antiquities, utensils, souvenirs, coins and wax impressions. In the two cases at the east end are clay, wood and plaster figures added by later Trevelyans, and some of the large geological collection made by

Sir Walter Calverley Trevelyan. The birds and eggs were Lady Wilson's, as were most of the shells at the west end of the room. The tropical fruits, fish, quadrupeds, fossils and bones in the fourth large case were also collected by Lady Wilson. On the walls are displayed two narwhal tusks, some saw-fish blades and war instruments from the south seas.

In the central case is a model of the Church of the Holy Sepulchre in Jerusalem as it was between 1554 and 1719. It was made by craftsmen in Bethlehem under Franciscan supervision, or by the Franciscans themselves.

Sculpture

Dr Henry Wentworth Acland (1815–1900) (plaster bust by Alexander Munro) was sculpted in 1857 to give thanks for his escape from the wreck of the steamship *The Tyne* in the Channel. He displayed immense courage throughout the ordeal, breaking down only when he discovered that his wife's Bible, prayerbook and portrait had been ruined by the storm. Acland was Munro's chief patron and a close friend of the Trevelyans and Ruskin.

(Right)
Dame Jane Wilson (1749–1818), who formed the cabinet of curiosities now at Wallington. She is shown holding the catalogue of her collection, with her family home, Charlton House in Greenwich, in the right background. The collection passed to her daughter Maria, who married Sir John Trevelyan, 5th Bt

(Left)
A puffer fish from Lady Wilson's Cabinet of Curiosities

27

The Garden and Park

The 18th-century creation

We know very little about the appearance of the garden and park before the remodelling of Wallington by Daniel Garrett for Sir Walter Blackett in 1738–40. Already by 1737 William Joyce, a Tyneside nurseryman, had drawn up a plan for landscaping the park and planting woods. In many ways the West and East Woods still follow this plan. Tributaries to the Wansbeck were dammed to form ponds, also still in existence, though the canal mentioned by the Duchess of Northumberland in about 1760 has been transformed into a series of ponds. The Garden Pond in the East Wood was originally part of an enclosed garden, the 'new kitchen gardens' described by Arthur Young as being

(Below) James Paine's bridge over the Wansbeck

'excellently disposed, kept in admirable husbandry'. In that garden still stands the charming Portico House, evidently designed by Garrett around 1740 and intended as a gardener's cottage. The West Wood was laid out with serpentine walks and arbours.

Another plan of about 1750 shows how the public road to Cambo was diverted from the west to the east of Wallington, as though to form a drive to the house. The Wansbeck was also dammed next to the proposed bridge, eventually built by James Paine in the Palladian style with a cascade below. In accordance with the fashion of the time, a Chinese pagoda was built beside what is still known as the China Pond, although this 'foolish expensive Chinese Building', in Mr Poynings's words, has long since disappeared. Between the China Pond and the Portico House wall there was a view across

the fields to 'The Arches', which formed the original triumphal approach to the house until moved to this now rather forlorn spot in 1754.

By the 1760s, the area round Rothley, two miles north-east of Wallington, had been enclosed as a deer-park, while on the crag above had been erected Sir Walter's most ambitious folly, a 'vast ruin'd Castle built of Black Moor Stone', designed by Garrett. Sir Walter had arranged in and around it Janus-headed busts and griffins' heads, obtained when Aldersgate and Bishopsgate in London were demolished. (They are now in the Walled Garden and on the East Lawn.) Rothley Castle was acquired by the National Trust in 2004.

Next he planned a 'fishing lake' and pleasure ground at Rothley, and for this he turned largely to 'Capability' Brown, who in the early 1760s had returned to Northumberland to work at Alnwick. Arthur Young thought the result 'noble': 'The bends and curves of the bank are bold and natural, and when the trees get up, the whole spot will be remarkably beautiful.' Thomas Wright of Durham's miniature fort nearby on Codger Crag, another eye-catcher, was built as a battery for five guns. 'Capability' Brown may also have designed the new kitchen garden in the dell beyond the East Wood. Facing south and well-sheltered, it is now known as the Walled Garden and is one of the great attractions of Wallington. Above this last was built the Owl House, a potting shed or bothy, so-called because it is surmounted by an owl, the crest of the Calverleys.

Victorian variety

Sir Walter Calverley Trevelyan and Pauline, Lady Trevelyan, as botanists and horticulturists, carried on the tradition of planting, introducing exotic conifers into the woods.

(Right) The Portico House

According to Edward Keith, who was head gardener from 1890 to 1933, 'His [Sir Walter's] greenhouses were filled with specimens of rare gems and otherwise from all parts of the world, a miniature Kew.' For vegetables Sir Walter preferred wild plants, such as sorrel and nettles, also edible fungi, which he ate for breakfast. He would never allow cut flowers in the house, or even flowers to be picked. He and Pauline Trevelyan were both particularly interested in ferns.

Sir Charles Edward Trevelyan, always impulsive and energetic, did much clearing of undergrowth in the woods. Sir Walter's exotic plants were ruthlessly sacrificed to make way for cut flowers for the London season. Sir Charles employed Edward Milner, an apprentice of

The Conservatory

Joseph Paxton, to design a formal parterre on the lawn between the house and the West Wood in 1882. The beds were filled with plants such as geraniums and lobelias. They proved to be a popular source of food for neighbouring deer, and may have looked too much like a municipal garden for the taste of his son, Sir George, who had them grassed over in 1906.

Edwardian abundance

It is to Sir George, who inherited Wallington in 1886, that we owe the main development of the Walled Garden. He imported terracotta urns and wrought-iron gates from Florence and Menaggio. The 18th-century lead figures were placed along the terrace of the Walled Garden, and Neptune was set above the entrance to this garden; hence the 'Neptune Gate'. Opulent herbaceous borders, keeping to the original shape of the dell, replaced greenhouses and vegetable beds. A rock garden and paths were made, and new greenhouses built, with a boiler on the level above. But the Conservatory or Winter Garden, completed in 1908, was Sir George's supreme contribution: an epitome of the Edwardian age. The scent of heliotrope almost overwhelms as you enter. Here still the descendants of his giant 'Rose of

(Right) The Mary Pool

Castile' fuchsias mingle with wall-trained geraniums, bougainvillea, abutilon, verbena, plumbago and *Senna corymbosa*.

Making the 'Mary Pool'

With the coming of war in 1914, improvements at Wallington necessarily ceased, and indeed were not resumed until after Sir George's death in 1928. The most important contribution to the garden in the next generation was the enlargement of the rockery at the west end of the

Walled Garden in 1938 to designs by Mary, Lady Trevelyan. She incorporated lots of old worked stone into the curved steps and water-garden pool, now named after her the 'Mary Pool'. Above this the National Trust has planted clematises, philadelphus and shrub roses. On either side are Japanese maples and honey-suckles. Sir Charles in 1939 commissioned Mr Creer of Belsay to make the Moscow Gate in the East Wood, which was based on a 16th-century Italian gate in Moscow. Both these improvements were made *after* the decision to give the property to the Trust. As Pauline Dower has written, he, like his grandfather, loved working in the woods, the children helping with clearing and making bonfires.

The garden today

The National Trust took charge of the garden when Sir Charles died in 1958. Although many changes have been made to the planting in the Walled Garden, the old part still has an 18th-century character, and the Winter Garden is almost exactly as it was in Sir George's day. Mauve *Erinus alpinus* grows in the brick walls

of the Walled Garden, which provide much-needed shelter in this severe climate for a remarkably wide range of plants. The border along the top path is planted with grey- and purple-leaved plants, including irises, Corsican hellebore and catmint.

In the 1960s and early 1970s the Trust's Gardens Adviser, Graham Stuart Thomas, redesigned the lower part of the Walled Garden, which had once been given over to vegetables. The old stream through the garden was re-established and edged with alpines and dwarf shrubs. He also created a broad new border sloping down towards the bottom of the garden, which was filled with phloxes, hostas and fuchsias against a background of large shrubs, arranged from pale to rich orange and red tones in Gertrude Jekyll style. Yew hedges enclose a small nuttery with spring bulbs and ornamental trees, while beyond and in contrast is a more open area with a new pond, where there had previously been derelict greenhouses. Overlooking this is a grove of *Acer lobelii*, planted in 1989 in memory of Pauline Dower. Wallington also contains the National Collection of Elders (*Sambucus*).

The Estate

The windswept ruins of Rothley Castle

When in 1728 Sir Walter Calverley inherited his uncle's estate at Wallington, it was largely moorland and, according to Sir Charles Philips Trevelyan, 'a conglomeration of ragged, unfenced crofts and pastures, enclosed by earth banks'. The only roads were cart tracks, and there were virtually no trees except patches of self-sown low timber at the bottom of gullies. All this is difficult to visualise now – in what seems to most visitors an ideal wooded land-scape with Shaftoe and Rothley Crags as contrasting backdrops. In less than 30 years Sir Walter Calverley Blackett (as he became) had fully established his 'noble and well-ordered estate'. Writing in 1767, the eminent agri-culturalist Arthur Young admired not only Sir Walter's new roads, as straight as if made by the Romans, but also the regularity of the whitethorn hedges, 'kept perfectly free from weeds'.

Sir Walter pulled down most of the medieval village of Cambo, leaving the 15th-century pele-tower with its thick walls. Originally the pele-tower was a watchtower against marauders from the north. He built a terrace of solid single-storey houses, known as the Front Row, for the men who worked his coal-mines in the Pit Field, west of Cambo Bank. (The second storey was added by Walter Calverley Trevelyan in the early 19th century.) At the end of the terrace, next to the road, Sir Walter Blackett also put up the Two Queens inn, which was completed in 1760. (The Queens were Elizabeth I and Mary Queen of Scots, who were then depicted on the sign.) Outlying cottages were also rebuilt and new farmsteads created.

The second Sir John Trevelyan built Holy Trinity church in 1842 at Cambo to designs by J. and B. Green, but for the last 20 years or so of his life he lived mostly in Somerset, so it is not surprising that his Northumberland estate began to suffer. His son, Sir Walter Calverley Trevelyan, at once set about improvements and restorations, spending £30,000 on new drainage. Every kind of new scientific invention or agricultural machinery fascinated Sir Walter, and he was ready for experiments, both in Northumberland and Somerset, often with success. He built more labourers' cottages and a station for the Wansbeck railway at Scots Gap. As one of the leading campaigners against alcoholism in the country, he abolished the Two Queens' licence to sell intoxicating liquor and opened a temperance hotel beside the new railway station at Scotsgap (now the National Trust North-East office). He laid out the Greenleighton plantation and the mile-long plantation east of Harwood. He also bought 8,000 more acres in the county, bringing the total estate to 22,000, and turned 2,000 acres into pasture for his prize Highland Kyloes. Towards the end of his life Sir Walter became more tight-fisted, and paid less attention to improving Wallington. In his long will with its sixteen codicils, he left Rothley Crag and separate properties to relatives.

In his seven-year tenure, Sir Charles Edward Trevelyan made considerable improvements to the estate for the benefit of his workers and ten-ants. He enlarged Cambo by building the Back Row, built two village schools, and turned the

old school into the village reading room. He added the tower to the church and gave it a clock and a peal of bells. His many new plantations include that on the east of the road up Cambo bank, and another north of Holyburn Lane, known as the Edward Grey plantation, after a successful day's shooting with the Foreign Secretary. Although his son, Sir George Otto Trevelyan, held Wallington for 40 years, he did little to the estate, apart from new drainage.

Sir Charles Philips Trevelyan, especially during the later years of his father's life, became impatient because he had never been consulted about the management of the estate, and could see that it was becoming seriously run down. As soon as he inherited the estate, he prepared a plan for the improvement of all the houses and farms to provide running water, baths and sewerage. He also installed electric light at Wallington and Cambo. He sold 1,500 acres to the Forestry Commission, and did a considerable amount of tree-planting on the remainder of the estate.

After the Deed of Settlement was signed with the National Trust in 1941 (see p. 55), there were inevitably some differences of opinion between Sir Charles and the Trust. For example, he gave a very long lease to the Forestry Commission of a considerable acreage in the northern part of the estate. He was legally entitled to do this, but he did so without telling the Trust, which was, to say the least, tactless. But neither Sir Charles nor the Trust wanted a row, and so the difficulties were smoothed over. In order to assist his tenant farmers in the difficult years before, during and after the Second World War, Sir Charles did not raise rents, as he could legally have done.

One of the Trust's first priorities, when it took over in 1958, was a new programme of modernisation, which had to be done with the help of government grants. Tree-planting was concentrated on the farmland in the centre of the estate, where shelter belts, so vital in this exposed countryside, were renewed and extended, mixing conifers and broad-leaved species.

In recent years conservation principles have assumed increasing importance. These have to be balanced against the general wish for greater public access and satisfactory returns from tenanted farms and woodlands. Access to the estate has been encouraged by three extended footpaths: in the Wansbeck valley; along the disused railway lines in the middle of the estate; and on the northern moors.

Wallington and its owners

The Fenwicks: bloodshed and hospitality

After the Norman Conquest Wallington was held by the barons Bolbec, who probably built the original castle. It stood on the site of the present house and seems to have consisted of a defensive pele-tower common in the troubled Border region in the Middle Ages.

Wallington features in many a Border ballad, and the Fenwicks, who inherited the estate in the early 15th century, were a formidable and pugnacious clan, ever ready to do battle against the Scots. 'A Fenwyke! A Fenwyke! A Fenwyke!' was their gathering cry. When the Percys were away at the Crusades, they were looked to for Northumberland's defence. 'Sound the bugle at Alnwicke, bag-pipe at Wallington! Wake the wild hills around,

The Jacobite Sir John Fenwick, 3rd Bt (1645–97), who sold Wallington to the Blacketts in 1688 and was executed for treason

summon the Fenwicke!' Then at the Raid of Reidswire on 7 June 1575:

We saw come marching owre the knowes
    Five hundred Fenwicks in a flock,
With jack, and speir, and bowes all bent,
    And warlike weapons at their will.

And afterwards:

Proud Wallington was wounded sair,
    Albeit he was a Fenwick fierce.

The 16th-century antiquary John Leland wrote of Wallington Castle as the 'chiefest howse of the Fenwiks', with Sir John Fenwicke as 'now lorde of it'. In the survey of 1542 it is described as a 'strong tower and stone house in good reparacions'. The Fenwicks, as a pun on their name, adopted the phoenix as their crest. Lead waterpipes, decorated with winged faces sometimes thought to relate to the phoenix, are still to be seen around the present building. The only other remains of their house are the cellars, where there are doorways hinged for heavy gates, narrow windows and a well that was used for water when moss troopers were roaming the countryside.

The Fenwicks were known for their convivial hospitality after a good day's chase. 'Show me the way to Wallington' was a favourite air in the neighbourhood:

Harnham was headless, Bradford breadless
    Shaftoe picked at the craw
Capheaton was a wee bonny place
    But Wallington banged them a'.

The Sir John Fenwick who was born in 1579 added greatly to the estate of Wallington, but in none too scrupulous a manner: he was described in 1617 as one of the 'greatest thieves in the county'. He bought a baronetcy in 1629 and as a Deputy Lieutenant of the county showed great energy in mustering forces for the King. In 1644 he was taken prisoner by the Parliamentarians, but, having made peace with them, was readmitted to the House of Commons in 1646. Three years later, there was an invasion by the Scots, and his estates suffered considerable losses.

His grandson, also Sir John Fenwick, was born in 1645 and was a great favourite at the court of Charles II, to whom he was adviser for his stables. He is said to have been the first to have produced the pure-bred British racehorse. A broad and steep track was flattened down to the Wansbeck from the front of Wallington, reputedly in order to exercise his thorough-breds, and is still known as the Gallop. He was elected to Parliament in 1678 and again in 1680, and by 1688 he was a major-general. However, shortly before the 'Glorious Revolution' which deposed James II in 1688, his wild extravagance had forced him to sell Wallington to Sir William Blackett, a wealthy Newcastle merchant and mine-owner, for £4,000 and an annuity of £2,000 for his and his wife's lifetimes.

Fenwick was a staunch Jacobite and behaved in a reckless and arrogant manner, persistently plotting against William III. In 1689 he was sent to the Tower, but on being released, at once resumed his hostile behaviour. He was the most conspicuous of those who swaggered along what came to be known as 'the Jacobites' Walk' in Hyde Park. He impudently cocked his hat in the face of Queen Mary and is said even to have spat on her train. As a result, the park-keepers were ordered to close the gates to him. In 1692 he was arrested again, after being implicated in a riot in Drury Lane. Once more he was released, but after being linked with another plot, went into hiding. He tried to flee abroad but was betrayed and caught. Having been summoned to the Bar of the House of Commons, he was condemned to death for high treason. Although he had been a 'faithless, tyrannical husband', his wife threw herself at the King's feet to beg for pardon, but it was no use. Since she was the daughter of the Earl of Carlisle, Fenwick was not hanged as a commoner, but beheaded on Tower Hill, in 1697. On the scaffold he produced a letter affirming his loyalty to James II and his legitimate heirs.

The Blacketts

The great riches of the Blacketts, based on shipping, collieries and lead-mines, were created by Sir William's father, also a Sir William. The first Sir William, whose family came originally from Durham, married a Northumbrian, Elizabeth Kirkley. Wealth brought political

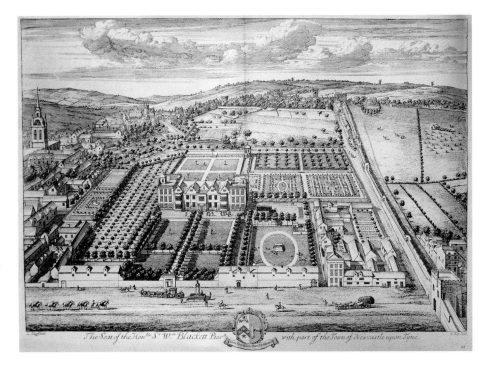

Anderson Place, the Newcastle mansion of the first Sir William Blackett, who founded the family fortunes; bird's-eye view, c.1700, by Kip and Knyff

The Seat of the Hon.ble S.r W.m Blackett Bar.t with part of the Town of Newcastle upon Tyne

power: he was Sheriff of Newcastle in 1660, Mayor in 1666 and Member of Parliament in 1673, the year in which he received a baronetcy. To cement his civic position, he bought Anderson Place in Newcastle, described as 'very stately and magnificent, and supposed to be the most so of any house in the whole kingdom within a walled city'. He embellished it still further by adding two wings and laying out the vast gardens and orchards which appear in Kip and Knyff's bird's-eye view (*c*.1700).

Sir William Blackett 'the Orator', builder of Wallington

The first Sir William died in 1680, leaving a large fortune to his eldest son Edward, who moved to Yorkshire and built the beautiful Newby Hall near Ripon in the early 18th century. The second son, Michael, died young. So it was the third son, William, who inherited the Northumberland estates and business interests which enabled him to buy Wallington from John Fenwick in 1688. He proved to be as powerful a commercial potentate as his father, representing Newcastle as a Whig in Parliament, where he was known as 'the Orator', and receiving a baronetcy in his own right.

'Not one to dawdle around or hesitate', he immediately pulled down the Fenwicks' house at Wallington and the medieval tower, leaving the ground floor as cellars. Using the old weathered stones, he built a new house, square in plan with four ranges 120 feet long around a central courtyard. Today visitors approach the house from the north and enter by the east front. Sir William arranged his house so that he could enter it on the south side directly off the old public road from Kirkharle to Cambo, which ran close by the west side of the house. The entrance and the main rooms, which included a great hall 44 feet long, were therefore placed on the ground floor of the south range. At each corner ladders instead of staircases rose to the first floor, which had no partitions or divisions. The north range contained the domestic offices, including the Servants' Hall and what is now the Common Room, where the original glass and wide glazing bars can still be seen in the

Sir William Blackett 'the Orator' (c.1657–1705), who bought the Wallington estate in 1688 and rebuilt the house (Needlework Room)

windows. The quadrangular plan, the provision of a great hall, and the absence of staircases and corridors all suggest how conservative Northumbrian building was at the end of the 17th century. However, as Sir William, who seems to have been his own architect, already owned Anderson Place and appears to have used Wallington mainly as a shooting-box, he may have considered fashionable grandeur unnecessary.

Sir William evidently kept up the Wallington tradition for hospitality, according to a popular song:

The wines of Wallington old songsters praise,
The Phoenix [Fenwick] from her ashes Blackett raise.

Sir William Blackett III

The second Sir William died in 1705. His son, yet another Sir William, then aged sixteen, showed less ability. There were rollicking times at Wallington, and six lackeys were kept to carry drunken guests upstairs. Following the family radition, when Sir William came of age, he was elected MP for Newcastle and remained so until his death.

In 1725 he married Lady Barbara Villiers, daughter of the 2nd Earl of Jersey. We are told that no fewer than 1,086 pairs of kid gloves – a traditional gift to wedding guests – were distributed for this event. There were also extraordinarily wild scenes, of all places on the summit of Shaftoe Crags between Wallington and Belsay. The basin in the rock known as the Devil's Punchbowl was enlarged. There were bonfires and a 'drink-maddened crowd' danced to a piper's tunes.

Sir William died in 1728. Perhaps the marriage to Lady Barbara was not a success, for it was childless, and she almost immediately remarried. At any rate it was revealed in his will that he had an illegitimate daughter, Elizabeth Ord, by then aged seventeen. The Wallington estate, Anderson Place and all the business interests went to his nephew, Walter Calverley, aged 21. But there was a condition. Walter had not only to marry Elizabeth within twelve months, but he must also take the arms and name of Blackett. The terms of the will were accepted, in spite of what might seem crippling debts of £77,000. In this way Sir William secured not only the survival of the family name, but also the social and financial position of his daughter.

Sir Walter Calverley Blackett

Walter was an energetic young man, ruddy complexioned and described as manly and well-proportioned, with a 'carriage erect and stately'. He had exceptional taste, and it is to him that we owe much of the Wallington that we see today. His wife, who died in 1759, remains a vague figure and is never mentioned in all the extravagant and inspired planning; the encomiums after her death speak only of her piety, purity of manners and bountiful charity. They had one child, a daughter also named Elizabeth, who died young. If Walter was reputed to have had a 'love of glory and display', and to have been noted for his 'courtly behaviour', he had no delusions of personal

grandeur. 'Every man carries his honour in his own hand,' he is reported to have said, 'origin is nothing; it shall never have any weight with me.' He took care of his workmen, 'in sickness, age or season of adversity'. Like previous Blacketts, he loved entertaining.

The house Walter inherited would have seemed inadequate for his needs, and around 1735 he began to think about improving it. He first built the low L-shaped ranges that lie either side of the central stable building. They were a simple exercise, and what gave him a taste for fashionable architecture was the library that he gave to St Nicholas's church in Newcastle in 1736. The façade of the building is copied from one of the best-known English sources for the

Sir Walter Calverley Blackett (1707–77), who transformed Wallington; portrait by Sir Joshua Reynolds (Drawing Room)

Sir Walter Calverley Blackett's remodelled house in 1777, the year of his death. Sir Walter inserted fashionable sash-windows, but retained the primitive outdoor privies (two are shown against the west front)

Palladian style, Lindsey House, Lincoln's Inn Fields. The architect was James Gibbs, one of the leading London architects of the day. It was not Gibbs (who was a Scot and a suspected Jacobite sympathiser), but Daniel Garrett, a close associate of Lord Burlington and the Palladian group (and a sound Whig) whom Sir Walter brought in to start alterations to Wallington in 1738. They consisted in turning the house round, reroofing it, inserting more fashionable sash-windows, rebuilding the north side and remodelling much of the interior. By the end virtually all that remained of the original house was the basic plan. The south front is the most interesting example of Garrett's remodelling. He doubled the height of the entablature, which he carried all round the house, and put on a simple pediment that stands proud of the hipped roof behind.

Garrett made a new principal entrance on the east side and built a new staircase hall on the south side of the quadrangle, in which he inserted a fine, but simple, double staircase. He also changed the proportions of the rooms in the south range, and made the three west rooms, one of which had been the staircase, into the main bedroom apartment. Hitherto one room had merely led into another; Garrett created a passage round the perimeter of the internal courtyard, thus reducing its size. He employed Italians, led by Pietro Lafranchini, for the superb plasterwork of sphinxes, garlands and fruit on the ceilings and walls of the Saloon and Dining Room. The plasterwork was done by 1743, and by the early 1750s the remodelling of the house was largely complete.

For some years there was a triumphal arch in the centre of the stables, but, since it proved too narrow for some carriages, this was removed to a field, to be turned into an eye-catching folly visible from the gardens by the China Pond. Its replacement, the present building known as the Clock Tower, is topped by a cupola on nine Doric columns and is one of the loveliest features of Wallington; it was completed in 1754, probably to designs for a chapel by Garrett, who had died the previous year. Walter then turned o another north country Palladian architect, James Paine, who built the splendid hump-backed bridge over the Wansbeck in 1755, to provide an eye-catcher and link with the public road, which was moved to the east side of the house (see p. 28). William Newton of Newcastle was responsible for most of Walter's later works at Wallington.

If Walter possessed the family flair when managing his multifarious business interests, he must also have been relying on the prospect of his future inheritance from his father to redeem his debts and truly tremendous expenses. For the income from coal and lead was fluctuating in an alarming way. His father did not in fact die until 1749. Over the following years the Yorkshire estates were therefore sold, raising £106,000, of which £70,000 was used for 'buying' Wallington from the trustees, presumably in connection with mortgages.

Sir Walter Calverley Blackett, as he became after his father's death, spent generously on others as well as himself. He contributed large sums to the poor of Newcastle and subscribed handsomely to a new infirmary. Hexham, because of the lead mines he owned at Allendale nearby, benefited from his charity perhaps most of all; among other things he built the market place and bridge there. He was High Sheriff of Northumberland in 1732 and five times Mayor of Newcastle.

Sir Walter also sat in the Commons without a break from 1734 until his death. The election in 1741 was especially memorable, when he was returned with Nicholas Fenwick (a distant kinsman of the Jacobite) as one of the two Tory representatives for Newcastle. His expenses were an amazing £6,319. Two blue-and-white punchbowls, still at Wallington, celebrate the event with the inscription, 'Lett us drink success to Blackett and Fenwick'. When Bonnie Prince Charlie invaded England in 1745, Sir Walter – in spite of his low opinion of George II – was 'indefatigable at Newcastle in consulting and providing for the safety of that town'.

Sir Walter transformed not only the house at Wallington but the whole estate (see p. 32). On hitherto undrained fells and moors, bridges were

The Clock Tower was built for Sir Walter Calverley Blackett, probably to designs by Daniel Garrett

erected, fields created and enclosed, labourers' cottages built in stone, woods planted, and the roads made suitable for stage-coaches. A possible witness of these improvements was Lancelot 'Capability' Brown, who was born in 1716 at Kirkharle, about two miles from Wallington, and went to school in Cambo. Working as a young gardener on the Kirkharle estate, he may have been aware of the alterations to the great house and the surrounding plantings before he went south in 1739. Very likely he gave additional advice on the latter when he returned for a while to Northumberland in 1765, and he certainly helped to create Rothley Lake as part of a new pleasure ground for Sir Walter. Sir Walter also made a series of ornamental ponds, filling them with tench and carp, in the East and West Woods. In his later years Sir Walter's favourite occupation after dinner was to drive up to Rothley Lake, or else feed the fish in the ponds nearer home.

'He had most of the virtues that cause a man to be beloved, and a large assortment of frailties which, in those far from Puritanical days, told rather for than against his personal popularity.' This intriguing and obviously discreet comment by an anonymous memorialist writing in 1819 is amplified by a letter in the Alnwick archives, undated but probably written in 1767, from one P. Poynings, in which he adds:

He is a Man of a very peculiar turn of Character. He is about 60 years of Age of a strong robust Make, and was call'd a handsome Man. He has been greatly addicted to Women but his Amours have been chiefly among Servant Maids & Women of that Class.

Mr Poynings considered that Sir Walter's fondness for his dogs was 'quite ridiculous and childish', and commented that he was a 'vrai Gourmand', eating voraciously,

although not a hard drinker. Sir Walter, having completed his fine mansion, park, follies and gardens, seems to have lost his zest for life:

He is call'd a jovial Companion and yet seems to have no satisfaction in anything. He loves to have his House continually full of Company yet seeming tired of them, himself and everything else. He is so good a Churchman that sick or well he never omits going to Church, but constantly sleeps the whole time he is there. Fishing and Shooting he seems to like, but within Doors (as he neither loves Study or Play) has no amusement. In a word he seems surrounded by all the Advantages of this Life without having any Relish for any of them.

Sir Walter died in 1777, aged 70. He left Wallington to the son of his sister Julia, Sir John Trevelyan, who was already the owner of some 20,000 acres in the south-west of England. Once again, the house passed through the female line.

The Trevelyans

The Trevelyans were originally Cornish, from St Veep above the River Fowey. The family coat of arms shows a white horse swimming, and this goes back to the legend that an ancestor escaped on a white horse from Lyonesse, the mythical kingdom beyond Land's End, after it was flooded. When, at the end of the 19th century, doubts were cast on the legend of

The first Trevelyan rides ashore at St Michael's Mount in Cornwall on a white horse – the origin of the family coat of arms. Molly Trevelyan spent 23 years making this needlework panel, which now hangs in the Drawing Room

Sir George Trevelyan, the 3rd Baronet and brother-in-law of Sir Walter Blackett of Wallington, is regarded with reason as the black sheep of the family. The 'wicked Sir George', as he was called, did a great deal of damage not only to the estate, but also to the family's reputation in Somerset. His father, a cultivated man, was horrified by his 'vanity, folly, vice, extravagance and ill-nature'. He quarrelled with his neighbours, including the Rector of Nettlecombe, who, he said, was spreading a rumour that he had murdered a bastard child. Notwithstanding this, the Rector's daughter Nancy Rugge became his mistress and was set up in the family house in Bath. Not surprisingly, his children were ashamed of him, and, like his unhappy wife, eventually moved away, living either at Sir Walter Blackett's London house in Curzon Street or at Wallington.

'Vanity, folly, vice.' Sir George Trevelyan, 3rd Bt (1707–68). His son John inherited Wallington from Sir Walter Calverley Blackett; portrait by Thomas Hudson (Dining Room)

Lyonesse, it was decided that the 'first' Trevelyan must have swum ashore on his horse for a wager from St Michael's Mount – as depicted in the great needlework panel embroidered by Mary, Lady Trevelyan for the Drawing Room at Wallington.

In the 15th century a Sir John Trevelyan came to prominence as a staunch, but wily, Lancastrian, who, unlike many of his allies, escaped execution. It seems that it was Chaucer's granddaughter, the Duchess of Suffolk, who arranged for his marriage to her cousin, Elizabeth Whalesborough, heiress of the elder branch of the Raleigh family with immense estates all over the south-west and in Wales. Elizabeth's dowry also included Nettlecombe in Somerset, which thereupon became the main seat of the Trevelyan family. The Trevelyans of Nettlecombe suffered greatly for their Royalist sympathies in the Civil War, but were rewarded with a baronetcy by Charles II after his restoration.

Sir John Trevelyan, 4th Bt

The eldest son, John, was very different in character from his father, but always remained on respectful terms with Sir George. In 1757 he achieved independence by marrying an heiress of Huguenot descent, Louisa Marianne Simond. She died in 1772, leaving a death-bed letter to her surviving children which shows her to have been a sweet-natured and intelligent woman. It is a matter of debate whether the long noses of many future Trevelyans were due to Huguenot or Calverley ancestry (or both).

Sir John Trevelyan, as he became in 1768 on his father's death, was much loved by his descendants, but is said not to have got on well with the local gentry in Northumberland. He soon found owning large estates at opposite ends of the country too much of a burden. So he decided to move back to Nettlecombe, where his father had left the farms in a miserable state. Indeed for the next hundred years each inheritor of the title had to decide whether to make Nettlecombe or Wallington their main base. The houses themselves were very different: Nettlecombe, mostly late Elizabethan, in a deep romantic valley; Wallington, classical, with its sweeping views and bracing climate. From 1780

that he had to be winched up to the gallery at Nettlecombe when he went to bed. He died aged 94 in 1828.

Sir John Trevelyan, 5th Bt

John Trevelyan the younger, eventually 5th Baronet, was of a quiet and studious disposition, but as a fashionable young man had enjoyed balls, concerts and theatres in London. He was very musical, composed songs and was a passable artist; he was also interested in agriculture, rare trees and ornithology. His politics differed from his father's, so he never stood for Parliament. He travelled in France and Italy on the Grand Tour and collected Dutch pictures. As soon as he heard of the fall of the Bastille in 1789, such was his enthusiasm that he dashed across to Paris. But by 1798, when Britain and France were at war, his early, idealistic view of the French Revolution had gone, and he raised the Wallington troop of cavalry to rebuff the threatened invasion, with himself in command.

Sir John Trevelyan, 4th Bt (1734–1828), who inherited Wallington in 1777, but lived mainly on his Nettlecombe estate in Somerset; portrait by George Romney (East Gallery)

Maria Wilson (1772–1851), painted around the time of her marriage in 1791 to John Trevelyan, later 5th Bt; by John Hoppner (Trevelyan Bedroom)

to 1796 Sir John was Tory MP for Somerset. When in 1791 his eldest son, also called John, married rich Maria Wilson, he gladly let him have Wallington and 2,000 acres in Northumberland, 'interfering little with family arrangements', but retaining control of the rest of the estate. Like many Trevelyans, he was interested in natural history, creating a museum and sending field notes on birds to the celebrated Newcastle engraver and illustrator Thomas Bewick. He was a particular friend of Josiah Wedgwood the potter. His portrait by Romney shows the sturdy unpretentiousness of an English country squire. His considerable girth, due to his love of good wine and food, and his gout – a family affliction – meant

He was one of the first members of the Royal Horticultural Society, founded in 1804 by John Wedgwood, son of Josiah. Leading scientists such as Sir David Brewster became his friends and guests at Wallington. His marriage to Maria Wilson was very acceptable socially, and she brought a large dowry, not only in cash but also furniture and an enormous and magnificent collection of porcelain, chiefly *famille rose* and *famille verte*, much of which is still on view at Wallington. Maria was good-looking, high-complexioned, also with a fine nose, and grew into a formidable *grande dame*, priding herself on her good taste, conscious of the power of her wealth (£40,000 a year at the end of her life) and loving Wallington passionately. She was the youngest daughter of General Sir Thomas Wilson and his remarkable wife, known to all as Dame Jane. A series of six deaths within 30 years had brought a huge fortune into her family, including the manor of Hampstead and Charlton House near Greenwich. Like the elder Sir John Trevelyan at Nettlecombe, who became a friend, Dame Jane had a museum or cabinet of curiosities, but hers was famous chiefly for its fossils, shells, stuffed birds and dried insects, to which she added her husband's collection of Italian bronzes and weapons from the South Pacific. She is still regarded as a pioneer coleopterist, or expert on beetles. Every summer, after she was widowed in 1798, she would set out on fossil-hunting trips in her coach (keeping an eye ever open for interesting land snails and beetles) with two long-suffering spinster sisters, the Misses Bant, who were made to keep diaries. In 1815 the sisters recorded that they had travelled 1,915 miles, perpetually on the move and lodging in inns, however humble, since Dame Jane disliked sleeping in other people's houses. When Dame Jane died in 1818, she left her cabinet of curiosities to Maria, her favourite daughter, and John Dobson was brought in to create a special museum for it at Wallington.

Beatrice Trevelyan, one of Maria's unconventional children, drawn by her sister Emma in the Drawing Room in 1827. She is looking at the large Chinese fishbowl which is still in this room

Maria and John Trevelyan had twelve children, three of whom died young. Nearly all were born at Wallington. The eldest son was christened Walter Calverley Trevelyan, known as Calverley, and his questing mind and interest in geology and botany as a boy made him closest to 'Grandmater', who introduced him and his best friend at Harrow, the photographer William Fox Talbot, to James Sowerby, the conchologist and botanist, and to Michael Faraday, then a pupil of Sir Humphry Davy. Most of the children were musical, and most hated being dragged away from Wallington, in spite of their mother's efforts to launch them in society. Conventional people considered them brusque, even rude, and 'careless in dress'. The younger girls had a habit of going into tenants' houses when they were out in the fields and rearranging the furniture to their liking. Few of the tenants dared object.

Servants found John Trevelyan very strict, and he is said to have personally horsewhipped an erring page. Things went badly between him and Maria. After his father retired permanently to Bath, he took over Nettlecombe's management, but she chose to stay at Wallington. When he travelled north, she travelled south, and vice versa; they used to meet at some pre-arranged spot and exchange family news through their carriage windows. However, after a while their sons and daughters 'compelled reconciliation'.

On both estates John planted quantities of trees, at Nettlecombe reckoned in thousands. He also created beautiful pleasure grounds at Nettlecombe, where scientific and horticultural friends were invited to meet like-minded neighbours. His great-uncle Sir Walter Blackett had determined that no vicar should live near Wallington, so the family church had been at Hartburn, five miles away. Now a large airy church was built at Cambo, completed in 1842 to designs by Benjamin Green. Very likely the supervision of all these works had been by Calverley, since by that time his aged father had gout and was less able to come to Wallington. Calverley was also endeavouring to run the Wallington estate, finding himself in constant conflict with his increasingly eccentric mother.

Sir John, as he became on the death of his father in 1828, died in 1846, aged 86. As for Maria, this 'masterful old dame' now had a two-wheeled 'chariot' drawn by two much-loved donkeys. She would sally forth from Wallington, with a burly liveried Irishman walking respectfully behind, and would point with a gold-tasselled cane at any of her son's shrubs or trees that offended her, and order her attendant to pull them up. She died in 1851 at Harrogate, where she habitually took the waters, and left a will which stipulated that the museum should be sold for the benefit of her 23 grandchildren. Calverley, who by now had himself accumulated many geological specimens, had to buy it back in its entirety. Dame Jane's china collection and the Charlton House furniture and books also remained at Wallington, after lawyers for the rest of the family had argued unsuccessfully that they formed part of the museum.

Sir Walter Calverley Trevelyan and Pauline, Lady Trevelyan

In 1835 Calverley had married Paulina Jermyn, nineteen years younger and in character very different from most of the Trevelyan family. Usually called Pauline, she was the daughter of a poor but learned Suffolk parson. She had attracted Calverley's attention at a meeting of the British Association for the Advancement of Science in Cambridge, when she was only seventeen. He, as a devotee of the new 'science' of phrenology, had noted with approval her 'anterior development'. Calverley (Sir Walter to the outside world after 1846, and Caly to Pauline) was tall, taciturn, with long hair and drooping moustache, and, unlike her, had a limited sense of humour. His energy was prodigious and he had a relentless thirst for knowledge – progress of any description, scientific or philosophical, appeared to magnetise him. As a geologist he was well-known, especially for his reports on his visit

Sir Walter Calverley Trevelyan (1797–1879); painted in 1839–41 by R.S. Lauder in romantic Walter Scott mode

the Faroe Islands. Antiquarians and fellow scientists, especially geologists such as Charles Lyell, his contemporary and friend at Oxford, respected him for his complete disdain of self-advertisement, and for the unselfish way he would undertake research for them, however arduous, and at his own expense.

Pauline was small, bright-eyed, brilliant, vivacious, teasing, artistic. She wrote poetry and painted, had a great gift for languages and considerable botanical knowledge. Her retentive memory and grasp of natural science amazed Cambridge dons. After the British Association meeting she transcribed almost word for word the long inaugural address by Professor Adam Sedgwick.

Until moving into Wallington in 1849, Calverley and Pauline lived mostly in Edinburgh. They also travelled much abroad, staying two years in Rome where Pauline was at the centre of expatriate intellectual life. She persuaded Calverley to buy Old Masters in Florence, including works attributed to Piero della Francesca and Luca della Robbia. Her sketches in Greece, based on Calverley's *camera lucida,* are now in the British Museum. Back in Edinburgh Pauline wrote for *Chambers's Journal* and reviewed books and art exhibitions for the *Scotsman,* while Calverley exhibited Fox Talbot's 'photogenic drawings'. She became a Tractarian; he was, on the contrary, 'strict' Evangelical. He was on several learned committees, attending lectures on subjects as varied as oxygen, urine, glaciers and parasites of starfish. He campaigned for state education, was a strong pacifist and against capital punishment, flogging, tobacco and opium.

In Rome Calverley had been known as the 'Apostle of Temperance' and he became an ardent teetotaller. On inheriting Nettlecombe he is said to have emptied wine from his father's cellar into a lake, though some was kept to be passed to suitable people 'for scientific purposes'. The Wallington cellars were kept locked and licences for liquor on the estate were

An 1854 drawing of the Swiss Alps by John Ruskin, who became a close friend of Pauline Trevelyan

abolished, although Pauline made sure that a decanter of wine (cheap) was available for guests. Intensely interested in modern farming methods of every description, he instituted deep drainage and 'brought land into a high state of cultivation', winning prizes with his Shorthorn and Red Kyloe cattle. He was said to have been 'personally acquainted' with each of his tenants, taking a fatherly interest in their welfare. He improved farmhouses and built up-to-date 'hygienic' cottages on both the Wallington and Nettlecombe estates; North Row at Cambo was an example of such improvements.

Pauline visited Turner's studio in London. She considered the first volume of Ruskin's *Modern Painters* (1834) a work of genius, and soon became a close friend of both Ruskin and his wife Effie. To Ruskin she was to be his 'monitress-friend in whom I wholly trusted'. She jokingly called him 'Master', and he helped her with her painting. Her circle grew to include the Pre-Raphaelites.

After 1849 Wallington became the main home for Pauline and Sir Walter, and her influence on the house is still strongly felt. In order to create a large new room for sociable family gatherings, it was decided to roof over the central courtyard, and John Dobson, the leading architect in the North-East, was called in. The work was held up until after Ruskin had been to stay in June 1853. Although Pauline was still recovering from a serious illness, which had entailed one of the first operations performed under chloroform, Ruskin told his father how:

Lady T. kept us laughing all day long . . . The pleasantness of these people consists in their very different qualities: in Lady Trevelyan in her wit and playfulness, together with very profound feeling; in Sir Walter in general kindness, accurate information on almost every subject, and the tone of mind resulting from a steady effort to do as much good as he can to the people on a large estate, I suppose not less than twenty square miles of field and moor.

Soon afterwards William Bell Scott, artist, poet and head of the government School of Design at Newcastle, was drawn into the world of Wallington. A comment by him on Pauline is

'A true woman, but without vanity.' Pauline, Lady Trevelyan (1816–66); painted by William Bell Scott in 1864

perhaps significant: 'She was a true woman, but without vanity, and very likely without the passion of love.' The Trevelyans were very close, despite their different temperaments, but their marriage was to be childless.

Scott was summoned to Wallington on 2 July 1855. 'As I approached the house,' he wrote, 'the door was opened, and there stepped out a little woman as light as a feather and as quick as a kitten, habited for gardening in a broad straw hat and gauntlet gloves, with a basket on her arm, visibly the mistress of the house.' Over the next two years a scheme of decoration by Scott for the Central Hall was discussed with the Trevelyans. The correspondence is vast. Eight historical scenes were to be painted, all on Northumbrian subjects and following the Pre-Raphaelite principles of truth to nature that his patroness admired. An introduction by Pauline to Ruskin was a failure, as both men disliked one another.

'Gruffly kind.' Sir Walter Calverley Trevelyan; painted by William Bell Scott in the Drawing Room in 1859

Most of Pauline's friends had nicknames: Scott, being prickly and jealous, was 'Mr Porcupine'. When she heard that the sculptor Thomas Woolner, one of the original seven of the PRB, had said that all people with titles were 'maggots', she at once set about 'taming' him and ordered medallions of Tennyson and Browning. Woolner soon became a friend, supplying her with a flow of gossip about writers and artists, particularly the Tennysons and Carlyle. Sir Walter had wanted tropical plants in the middle of the Hall, but having noted at the Crystal Palace that such things were 'conducive to damp', was persuaded by Pauline that Woolner should provide a marble group that would be the 'crown and centre of all that the pictures tell'. After much discussion the subject chosen was a mother teaching her child the Lord's Prayer: 'a simple act of purity, devotion and mother love, symbolising Civilisation itself'. It would stand on a plinth with contrasting scenes of barbaric violence in ancient times, such as cannibalism and Druidic sacrifice. To the childless Pauline the choice must have had a certain poignancy.

She herself had set about painting flowers and plants on the pilasters, aided by her great friends Laura Capel Lofft ('Phluff') and Mrs Mark Pattison, later Lady Dilke ('Piggy'). On Ruskin's second visit to Wallington, in July 1857, he refused to paint the Annunciation Lily on his pilaster, as requested, but instead chose wild oats, wheat, cornflowers and yarrow, which, even though unfinished, is one of the loveliest aspects of the room. Other guests included the young Algernon Swinburne, whose grandfather lived at Capheaton a few miles away. It was at Wallington that Swinburne

originally 'breathed the air faintly laden with Pre-Raphaelite incense'. Pauline is regarded as the first to have recognised his genius and actually to have encouraged him to write.

As well as the new Central Hall, the Trevelyans converted the drawing room into a library. Cabinets were also created from old panelling to display Maria's collection of china. But little was done to modernise the house. Augustus Hare described the disadvantages of staying at Wallington in the early 1860s. He wrote of:

endless suites of huge rooms only partly carpeted and thinly furnished with ugly, last century furniture . . . If Sir Walter found the place papered and furnished like those of other people he would certainly pine away from excess of luxury. His hostess seemed hardly concerned with her guests' comfort, feeding them solely on artichokes and cauliflowers.

(Right) The Central Hall, which Calverley and Pauline Trevelyan enclosed and William Bell Scott decorated with murals of Northumbrian history

Later Hare found Sir Walter 'gruffly kind and grumpily available'. 'As to information he is a perfect mine and knows every book and every ballad that was ever written, every story of local interest that was ever told, and every flower and fossil that was ever formed.' Pauline he found a 'pleasant bright little woman with sparkling black eyes, who paints beautifully'. She was also 'abrupt to a degree, and contradicts everything'.

She died on 13 April 1866, aged only 50, at Neuchâtel, where she was buried. Her husband and Ruskin had sat at each side of her deathbed. As Ruskin wrote to his mother: 'She was an entirely pure and noble woman, and had nothing to think of that day except other people's interests.' She was worrying about Swinburne only a few hours before her death. A year after Pauline's death Calverley married her friend Laura Capel Lofft, both believing that they were making a symbolic union in her memory. The new Lady Trevelyan was very stout, highly strung and played the organ excruciatingly in the Central Hall. She disliked Swinburne, and gradually the artistic circle created by Pauline at Wallington dissolved.

Sir Walter's cousin, Sir Charles Edward Trevelyan (who was himself created a baronet for his government works), had learnt in 1863 that he was to inherit Wallington, in an almost casual postscript to a letter from Sir Walter otherwise concerned with the evils of alcohol. Sir Walter and Pauline had some time back been impressed by his son George Otto's lively self-assurance and radical political enthusiasms (see p. 50). Since Nettlecombe was entailed to the next heir to the original baronetcy, that estate went to Sir Walter's nephew, Alfred Trevelyan, but Sir Walter legally broke the entail on Wallington. He had, moreover, long decided, as he told Sir Charles, that it was 'bad for the country' for any one individual to hold such sizeable possessions so far away from one another.

Sir Walter died on 23 March 1879, his wife of a heart attack the day after. Sections from his museum were dispersed in his will to the Oxford and British Museums and other learned institutions, but some remained and are shown in the cabinet of curiosities. When the cellars of Wallington were opened, some 60 dozen bottles of rare wines were found buried in fungus and cobwebs, including a 1745 sherry, presumably laid down for the Duke of Cumberland after the battle at Culloden, and magnums of hock left over from Calverley's grandfather's 1777 electoral victory celebrations.

Sir Charles Edward Trevelyan

Sir Charles Trevelyan was able to enjoy Wallington for only seven years, but enjoy it he did. All the energy, all the enthusiasm that had marked his stormy career now went into improving the estate and the lot of those who lived there. He was the son of Sir Walter's uncle, the Ven. George Trevelyan, Archdeacon of Taunton, and Harriet Neave, daughter of a Governor of the Bank of England. As his grandson G. M. Trevelyan was to write: 'He was

'A man of rigid integrity.' Sir Charles Edward Trevelyan (1807–86), who inherited Wallington after a career as a hard-working civil servant; portrait by Eden Eddis

ne of those utterly fearless and disinterested
men, who have their own standards and always
ct upon them.' Trollope satirised him as Sir
Gregory Hardlines in *The Three Clerks* (1857).
Macaulay said: 'He has no small talk. His mind is
all of schemes of moral and political improvement, and zeal boils over in his talk. His topics
even in courtship are steam navigation, the
education of the natives, the equalization of
the sugar duties.' He also added: 'He is a man
of genius, a man of honour, a man of rigid
integrity, and of a very kind heart.'

Charles began his career in the Indian civil
service and at the age of 22 denounced his
superior, the Resident at Delhi, for corruption.
He played an important part in the 'Great
Game', the rival manoeuvrings between Russia
and Britain in north-west India. With Macaulay,
whose sister Hannah he married at Calcutta in
1834, he fought successfully for the adoption
of English as the *lingua franca* in the Indian
sub-continent. Immensely hard-working, he
would sometimes be in the office by 4am.

Whilst at the Treasury he was in charge of
relief during the Irish Famine of the 1840s,
He visited Ireland and showed great sympathy
for the starving, organising relief in accordance
with his own high standards and those of
successive British governments, with total
integrity. He has been attacked, not always
justly, for not having done more to help the
victims of the Famine.

With Sir Stafford Northcote he was responsible, after much controversy, for the reform
of the Civil Service, replacing patronage with
competitive examinations. He became
Governor of Madras, but was recalled after a
clash with the central government. Notwithstanding this, he was appointed Finance Minister
at Calcutta, where he managed mostly to
restrain himself in spite of strong disagreements.

Charles received the KCB for his work
during the Irish Famine and a baronetcy in 1874.
Hannah had died the year before, and in 1875 he
married Eleanora (Nora) Campbell. Dark-haired
when young with those strong Huguenot, or
Calverley, features, he was remembered as
squire of Wallington in his seventies for 'his tall,
wiry frame, his snow-white hair, his face as

*'Dainty.' Lady Eleanora Campbell (1829–1919), the
second wife of Sir Charles Trevelyan. She refurnished the
house after he inherited in 1879*

rugged as a sea-worn rock, its deep lines instinct
with energy and power, his eyes alive for everything happening'. Having been a great pig-
sticker in India, he now became passionately
keen on shooting grouse, pheasants and black-
cock. He tackled every problem on the estate
with enormous zest. Often before breakfast he
would be seen galloping at full speed, coat-tails
flying, on his way to give workmen instructions.
He planted shrubs and trees, not always in the
wisest places, made new flower-beds and
established order and 'beautified the unsightly
spots that marred both Wallington and Cambo
village'.

Walter Trevelyan's nephew, Alfred, had
expected to inherit Wallington and thus bitterly
contested his will. He was unsuccessful, but
landed Sir Charles with heavy legal fees. In

addition there were mortgages of £33,000 still outstanding at Wallington from the days of the Blacketts. Sir Walter had left the contents of the house, including Pauline's art collection, to Alfred, with the exception of the china, family portraits, the Calverley needlework and screen, and a proportion of the books in the Library. Eleanora therefore had to set about refurnishing the house completely. Like her predecessor Pauline, she was a tiny woman, considered 'dainty'; she was also very near-sighted and often described as 'trotting after' her husband, calling 'cuckoo, cuckoo' when she lost sight of him. Some of the new furniture was continental, which accounts for the unusual amount of Dutch pieces in the house, and these were obtained from the Duveen brothers of Hull, uncle and father of the art dealer. Other objects brought to Wallington had belonged to Macaulay, including his four-poster, now in the Trevelyan Bedroom, which had been Pauline's boudoir. Many of Macaulay's books are also in the Library, some marked with bloody finger-prints as he liked to read while shaving.

The last time Sir Charles left Wallington was typical of the man. Ten minutes before rushing to catch the train south, he was cutting back branches from an old yew above the ice-house.

Sir George Otto Trevelyan

Charles's son George Otto Trevelyan inherited the baronetcy and Wallington in 1886, at the age of 48. Slight, dark-haired, high-spirited, without that characteristic nose and looking rather more Macaulay than Trevelyan, he had features described as manly and expressive. He had charm and a sharp, erudite sense of humour, and had been very close to his uncle Lord Macaulay, but admitted that Pauline had tolerated him as an intelligent philistine. His early letters show him to have been brimming with self-confidence, as if the world was waiting for him to conquer it. He was head boy at Harrow and won the English prize three years running. His youngest son G. M. Trevelyan wrote that when he went up to Trinity, Cambridge, he was like a man entering his

inheritance. In 1862 he went to Calcutta as his father's secretary. This resulted in two best-selling books: *The Competition Wallah,* still the outstanding picture of the British in India in the mid-19th century; and *Cawnpore: The Story of a Massacre* (seven relatives had died at Cawnpore during the Indian Mutiny). In 1865 George was elected Liberal MP for Tynemouth, having bought the Chirton estate in Northumberland for £65,000, towards which Sir Walter put up £10,000, to secure the necessary residential qualification. This does admittedly seem an odd way to launch a career as a radical, and he seemed afterwards to have been ashamed of it. At the height of the struggle over the 1867 Reform Bill he wrote a political satire, *Ladies in Parliament,* which was widely circulated and laughed over. An enthusiast for Italian liberty, he rushed out the same year, hoping to be present at Garibaldi's attack on Rome.

'A busy, pushing man'. Sir George Otto Trevelyan (1838–1928), historian and politician; cartoon by Spy (Sir Leslie Ward), 1873 (National Portrait Gallery)

The Conservatory was created by Sir George Otto Trevelyan

About this time he fell in love with Caroline Philips, the daughter of Robert Needham Philips, a bluff and wealthy cotton merchant from Manchester and Liberal MP for Bury. Their love letters are delightful, full of hope and plans for building a life together. It was indeed to be a perfect marriage, lasting for nearly 60 years, until they died within a few months of one another. There were three children, in some ways very different in character: Charles Philips the Labour politician, Robert Calverley the poet, and George Macaulay the historian. They all grew up to love Wallington and their mother's lady's maid and later their nurse, Mary Prestwich (affectionately known as 'Booa'), who was a key figure in the household. Well into their teens they would spend hours on the floor of the Museum at Wallington playing their elaborate war-game *Kriegsspiel* with thousands of lead soldiers. G. M. Trevelyan said that he derived his fascination with military history from these games.

In 1868 George Otto became MP for the Border Boroughs in Scotland, a constituency only 40 miles from Wallington and which he loved for its associations with Sir Walter Scott, the Border ballads and Jacobite rebellion. Gladstone made him Civil Lord of the Admiralty, but he resigned because he opposed state grants to church schools. This was the first of his resignations; like his father, he was not one for compromise. 'A busy, pushing man is Mr Trevelyan,' went the caption to a Spy cartoon in *Vanity Fair*:

He can scarcely find life long enough for all the forms of activity in which he would indulge. He is in every 'movement' . . . For ever writing, speaking, questioning, moving, dividing, agitating, he has, so far, seen his labours bear no inconsiderable fruit.

Inspired and coached by his father, he fought for the abolition of the purchase system in the Army, and against monopolists and owners of ground rents in London. Socially a Whig, he became a radical in politics, agitating for the enfranchisement of the working class.

During the years of Liberal opposition he worked on his *Life and Letters of Lord Macaulay*, which was published in 1876 and became an immediate success. In 1880 his *Early Life of Charles James Fox* appeared, a brilliant and still admired book which decided Gladstone to let him return to the Admiralty. Two years later, after the murder of the previous Chief Secretary for Ireland in Phoenix Park, Dublin, he was offered and accepted the post. On George Otto's return from Ireland he was made Chancellor of the Duchy of Lancaster, and in 1885 became Secretary for Scotland, but resigned from the government once again, this time opposing complete Home Rule for Ireland.

After his defeat at the Border Boroughs the same year, he soon found himself disillusioned by the Unionist party, which he saw as contemptuous of all members of the Empire who were not Anglo-Saxons. So back he went to the Liberals and to government, risking attacks for being a political weathercock. In

1897 George Otto, Sir George now, decided to retire from public life, to enjoy his country estate and continue with his literary career. His wife 'Carry' had inherited an enormous neo-Elizabethan mansion, with mullioned windows and a forest of chimneys, near Stratford-on-Avon, called Welcombe, with 4,000 acres. So the owner of Wallington was once more in charge of another large and faraway property.

Generally, the Trevelyans spent the summers at Wallington and the winters travelling in Italy and at Welcombe, which was so big that they used only part of it. Wallington, which, as Carry's delightful watercolours show, in those days was covered with creepers, remained their main home.

Sir George kept a notebook of changes and improvements at Wallington. In 1887 he recorded rearranging the china collection, 'a long and delightful labour of love'. The furniture that he had inherited from Macaulay, including the desk on which he had written the *History of England*, was brought from London. Caroline was an enthusiast for William Morris designs, and bought Morris wallpapers, materials and tiles. Peacock-pattern curtains and chair covers were put in the Drawing Room. She also embroidered fire-screens and cushion covers. To replace Pauline's Italian pictures and complement the Morris decoration, paintings by Francia, Burne-Jones, Leighton and Watts were bought. In 1889 Sir George proudly wrote:

On the 5th March we paid off the last mortgage of Wallington, £22,190. Wallington is therefore free for the first time since 1690, and possibly long before. The Wallington mortgages have been paid off by Macaulay's copyrights, and *Life and Letters*.

The large Wallington library was a particular enjoyment for Sir George. 'He read the Greek, Latin and English classics with an avidity rare even among scholars.' He would read aloud to Caroline and the boys, who, like him, also loved the rough shooting on the moors, 'poking about with a gun'. He travelled in Italy often, once with Ruskin, and brought back wrought-iron gates and terracotta urns for the garden. Lady Trevelyan meanwhile would be at work with her watercolours. In London in the 1880s and '90s she was a leading Liberal hostess,

described as a 'little lady, standing very upright, moving very quietly and with dignity', always beautifully dressed in heavy silk, soft greys or blue, in later years with a lace cover on her head.

Sir George was a 'hearty Protestant but did not understand Christianity'. Nevertheless he went regularly to Cambo church, where he read the lessons. On 3 April 1903 he recorded, 'This day I gave up wine for good', which meant that it was cider only for guests. During the South African war of 1899–1902 he had sympathised with the Boers. He also supported the suffragettes. In 1899 he had published the first volume of his *American Revolution*, which put him in touch with a number of distinguished Americans, including Theodore Roosevelt, who stayed at Welcombe. He received the freedom of Glasgow and Dundee, and turned down Asquith's offer of a peerage. He was, however, delighted to be awarded the OM.

With the approach of old age he seemed to dread visitors. It was said that the house smelled and looked like a cathedral, because of the paraffin lamps and fading paintwork. After 1916 Sir George never went again to London. Parties were given for local people, but gradually Sir George retreated into a shell, concentrating on his grandchildren and children of old friends, and on his jigsaws. His eldest grandchild Pauline was particularly close, listening entranced as he read from the *Iliad* and *Odyssey* in the original Greek. Sir George and Caroline became inseparable: 'They had grown into one another, in mind and habit.' Both died in 1928, Caroline at Welcombe and Sir George, after travelling north with difficulty, at Wallington aged 90. Obituarists described him as a radical aristocrat. Wallington then entered a new, exciting phase of development.

Sir Charles Philips Trevelyan

The future Sir Charles Philips Trevelyan, 3rd Baronet of Wallington, began his political career aged 22 in 1892, as secretary to Lord Houghton, Lord Lieutenant of Ireland – a job he did not enjoy. His sympathies were radical, already then more so than his father's. Like his formidable andfather and namesake, he had a high and unflinching sense of duty, and relished being in opposition to the established classes. But unlike his two brothers, he was more interested in politics than literature. Educated at Harrow and Trinity College, Cambridge, he was handsome, black-haired, with piercing blue eyes, energetic, 'rough in mind and spirit', not one to make conversation.

In 1898 Charles went round the world with Sidney and Beatrice Webb. He loved the experience, especially in America where, because of his father's books, he was especially welcomed. From 1899 until 1918 he was Liberal member for Elland in Yorkshire. He wanted a wife who was 'thoughtful, serious and with strong moral courage', and in 1904 married Mary, or Molly, Bell, eleven years younger and just that. She was the daughter of Sir Hugh Bell of Rounton Grange, near Northallerton, a Teesside ironmaster and patron of the Arts and Crafts architect Philip Webb. Her half-sister was Gertrude Bell, the famous traveller and archaeologist in the Middle East. James Lees-Milne described Molly in later middle age as 'tall, poised, bustling', with pince-nez; others said that she looked as if she had stepped straight from a Victorian novel. She was also very musical.

Charles was concerned in the movement to open the moors and mountains to the public, and lived to see much of what he had fought for carried out. In 1901 he became Master of the 'Man Hunt', an exacting game of hare and hounds over the Lakeland fells, which was invented by his brother George and Geoffrey Winthrop Young, and continues to this day. For a while he was a Liberal Imperialist, and as such fell out with his father by supporting the British cause during the Boer War. He wanted the abolition of the House of Lords, and campaigned for Irish

Independence and tariff reform. He was on the Russian Committee, exposing persecutions by the Tsar and aggression in Persia. In 1908 he became Parliamentary Secretary of the Board of Education. His views were becoming strongly to the left and in favour of more state control. By now an anti-Imperialist, and having for some years been entirely out of sympathy with the government's foreign policy, he resigned on the declaration of war in 1914. With Ramsay MacDonald and others, he formed the Union of Democratic Control, advocating peace by negotiation. His unpopularity led him to lose his seat in 1918, and to the distress of his parents he joined the Labour Party.

In 1922 Charles was elected Labour MP for the Central Division of Newcastle. When Labour came to power in 1924, he was President of the Board of Education. It was said that nobody could have questioned his idealism and sincerity, but – once more like his grandfather – he was intolerant of other people's opinions and somewhat lacking in tact. He was also very active in support of the Soviet Union.

Until Charles inherited Wallington, the family divided its time between London and a house at Cambo, where guests included writers, politicians and theatre people. In London there would be political parties for up to 50. In the early years of her marriage Molly worked hard to help her husband, but later her energies were

(Right) The engagement photograph of Charles Philips Trevelyan and Mary Bell, September 1903

more concentrated on maternal and social duties, as prospective châtelaine at Wallington. She was, however, a leading light in the WLF, the Women's Liberal Federation. She formed a small choir and a company of Girl Guides on the estate, and in the 1920s was an active member of the Rural Women's Organisation. She was also one of the founders of the Women's Institute movement and on the national executive.

Charles and Molly's six children were brought up in the same spirit. They took it in turns to have lunch with their grandparents on Sundays, when jigsaw puzzles and readings from the classics were the main entertainments. They soon became conscious that some of their country neighbours looked askance at Charles's unconventional views, regarding him as a traitor to his class. 'We were absolutely outrés,' one of his children has said, 'we never went anywhere.' Their friends were very much of their own

Geoffrey Trevelyan canvassing for his father, Charles, who was standing as Labour candidate for the Central Division of Newcastle in 1923

intellectual standards and interests, from London or school.

Wallington was in poor repair when Charles and Molly took over in 1928. 'We had a feeling,' Molly wrote, 'that the house was awaiting a time of reawakening after many years of somnolence.' They all gathered in the Central Hall to give a great shout, to disperse the ghosts – luckily unaware of the precarious condition of the roof. (A surveyor later reported that even a loud noise might have brought it crashing down.) During the winter and spring of 1928–9 the roof of the Central Hall was removed and replaced, part of the outside wall of the Kitchen was rebuilt, and additional bathrooms and an improved hot-water system were installed. An electricity-generating station was also built to light the house and the village. At the same time Sir Charles dispensed with all menservants in the house. From Easter 1929 parts of the house were opened to the public at weekends in the afternoons, free of charge. In 1934 700 people visited the house and grounds between Easter and October. Discussion groups and study weekends for young people of radical views were also held at Wallington, and the first Youth Hostel in Northumberland was opened in the stables.

The Visitors' Book from 1929 to 1950 includes many famous names in the Labour movement: Stafford Cripps, Aneurin Bevan and Jennie Lee, Frank Wise, the party's General Secretary (who died at Wallington), Hugh Dalton, Michael Foot, Hugh Gaitskell, Barbara Castle, Clement Attlee. There were always political friends staying at the time of the Miners' Gala at Durham. From the world of the arts and letters, visitors included George Bernard Shaw, Sir Lewis Casson and Dame Sybil Thorndike (frequently), and E. M. Forster. In 1929 101 people came to stay, in 1934 160.

The Central Hall was the main place for entertainments, including tenants' parties. Although cider was again the only alcoholic drink, to some extent gaiety was back, with a great deal of country dancing and charades. Two grand pianos were put in the Saloon, now known as the Drawing Room, where eventually Molly's tapestry of the 'first' Trevelyan on his white horse was hung – it had taken 23 years to ish. The Library became the family room and re after dinner there were high-powered ord games, guessing games, Mah-jong and cing Demon, and guests could write poems the family bathroom wall.

In 1929 Sir Charles was back in government ain as President of the Board of Education. He voured co-education and introduced a bill for ising the school leaving age to fourteen and ving grants to parents on low incomes. When s bill was rejected because of expense in a time f slump, he applied his proposed measures on is own estate. In 1930 he was made Lord ieutenant of Northumberland – which found ttle favour in the county. This appointment e regarded as a means of improving the nagistracy, particularly by encouraging very lderly incumbents to retire. In 1931 he gave p political life, believing that his Labour colleagues were not sufficiently socialist; he was ater to be expelled from the party.

Sir Charles lent a large sum, reputedly £70,000, to the Soviet government (it was repaid) and could see no fault in the Soviet system, even after a visit to Russia in 1935 and another in 1938. He turned a blind eye, it was said, to what he did not care to see. What he did see was the supreme goal of no private profit: nobody enriched himself from the labour of others – you lived for the state. In 1934 he decided to settle Wallington, with its contents and all the estate, now about 11,500 acres, on the National Trust, with the proviso – in general terms – that the Trevelyan family should continue to live in it. Such an offer had never before been made to the Trust, and negotiations lasted some years. In July 1935 Lord Lothian, a friend and the owner of Blickling in Norfolk, made an historic speech about the need to preserve the best of England's ancient estates, and this gave added support to Sir Charles. From the beginning, Sir Charles discussed his plans within his family.

G. M. Trevelyan, who was Chairman of the Trust's Estate Management Committee and had given covenants along the Roman Wall, was enthusiastic. Sir Charles explained to his eldest son George that under the National Trust there would be more chance of Wallington being lived in for many years by the family than if he had left it to him:

At best you would have been unable to keep up the place properly, and with the certainty that when you died the property would be largely dispersed. The old order is crumbling, and the chance for the Trevelyans is actually better for remaining at Wallington under what I propose.

On 23 March 1937 Sir Charles, having first informed his tenants at Wallington, broadcast his intentions to the nation: 'As a Socialist, I am not hampered by any sentiment of ownership. I am prompted to act as I am by satisfaction at knowing that the place I love will be held in perpetuity for the people of my country.' The negotiations with the Trust resulted in the Deed of Settlement signed by Sir Charles in 1941. By this deed, Sir Charles effectively remained the life-tenant of Wallington and its estate, and after his death the National Trust became his irrevocable heir. When a daughter asked Sir Charles why he did not want the Trust to take over before his death, he said, 'Because I'm an illogical Englishman,' which she thought aptly summed up his life.

The terms of the settlement agreement, perhaps inevitably, brought problems with the Trust during the last seventeen years of Sir Charles's life, but his enthusiasm and enjoyment of Wallington were always evident, and he continued to love working in the woods. He was a warm and welcoming host, always encouraging the young, and after his death in 1958 there were discussions about various educational possibilities for the house, but by the time of Molly's death in 1966 those had been abandoned. The National Trust continued to open the house and gardens, and undertook redecorations between 1968 and 1971. The family link is maintained, with Sir Charles's youngest daughter, Patricia Jennings, still living in the house (and playing her Northumbrian pipes to visitors) and other descendants living at Wallington and nearby Cambo.

In the spring of 2004 the National Trust completed a major refurbishment and restoration of the house, including re-slating the roof, installing an up-to-date electrical system and considerable redecoration.

Owners of Wallington

Owners of Wallington
are in CAPITALS

Asterisk denotes
portrait in the house

Sir William = (1) Elizabeth Kirkley
Blackett, 1st Bt* (d. 1674) m. 1645
(c.1620–80) (2) Mary Cock
Newcastle (d. 1710)

Sir Christopher = (1) Elizabeth Langhorne
Conyers, 2nd Bt* (1628/9–54) m. 1648
(1621–93) (2) Hon. Julia Lumley
m. 1666

Sir Edward Blackett 2nd Bt (1649–1718) Matfen line

Michael (d. 1683)

Sir WILLIAM BLACKETT = (2) Julia Conyers* = (2) Sir William Thompson, M
1st Bt of 2nd creation* m. 1684/5 (1668–1739) m. 1711
(c.1657–1705)
Builder of Wallington

Sir WILLIAM BLACKETT 2nd Bt (1690–1728) = Lady Barbara Villiers m. 1725

Isabella (d. 1763) = Earl of Buchan m. 1743

Julia Blackett* (1686–1736) m. 1706/7 = Sir Walter Calverley, 1st Bt* (1669–1749)

Frances* = Hon. Robert Bruce m. 1729

Diana* (d. 1742) = Sir William Wentworth 4th Bt m. 1720

Anne* (d. 178 = (1) John Trenchard (2) Thoma Gordo

Elizabeth Ord (1711–59) m. 1729 = Sir WALTER CALVERLEY BLACKETT, 2nd Bt* (1707–77) assumed Blackett name 1733

Julia Calverley (1706–85) m. 1733 = Sir George Trevelyan 3rd Bt of Nettlecombe* (1707–68)

Gen. Sir Thomas Spencer Wilson, Bt (1723–98) = Jane Weller of Charlton Park* (1749–1818) m. 1767

Elizabeth* (1735–52)

Sir JOHN TREVELYAN 4th Bt* (1734–1828) = Louisa Simond (1734–72) m. 1757

Susanna 'Sukey' Trevelyan* (b. 1736) = John Hudson m. 1764

Walter (1743–1819)

Charles* (1744–88)

3 dau

Maria Wilson* (1772–1851) m. 1791 = Sir JOHN TREVELYAN 5th Bt* (1761–1846)

Walter (1763–1830)

The Ven. George Trevelyan (1764–1827) Archdeacon of Taunton = Harriet Neave (1773–1854)

Willoughby (1767–85)

4 sons

2 daus

Sir WALTER CALVERLEY TREVELYAN, 6th Bt* (1797–1879) = (1) Paulina Jermyn* (1816–66) m. 1835 (2) Laura Capel Lofft (1804–79) m. 1867

11 other children

Trevelyans of Nettlecombe

Sir CHARLES EDWARD TREVELYAN 1st Bt of Wallington* (1807–86) = (1) Hannah More Macaulay (1810–73) m.1834 Sister of Lord Macaulay* (2) Eleanora Campbell (1829–1919) m. 1875

5 sons

3 daus

Sir GEORGE OTTO TREVELYAN, 2nd Bt* (1838–1928) = Caroline Philips* (1849–1928) m. 1869

Sir CHARLES PHILIPS TREVELYAN, 3rd Bt* (1870–1958) = Mary Bell* (1881–1966) m. 1904

Robert Calverley Trevelyan (1872–1951) = Elizabeth van der Hoeven (1874–1957)

George Macaulay Trevelyan (1876–1962) = Janet Ward (1879–1936)

Pauline (1905–88)

Sir George Lowthian Trevelyan, 4th Bt of Wallington, 10th Bt of Nettlecombe (1906–96)

Katharine (1908–90)

Marjorie (1913–2003)

Florence Patricia (b. 1915)

Sir Geoffrey Washington Trevelyan, 5th Bt of Wallington, 11th Bt of Nettlecombe (b. 1920)